The Savvy
Tax Payer
Playbook:

Winning Strategies for Beating the IRS

at Their Own Game

By
Mack O'Hara

The Savvy Tax Payer Playbook:
Winning Strategies for Beating the IRS at Their
Own Game

Disclaimer

The information contained in this book is for general information purposes only. The author and publisher make no representations or warranties of any kind, express or implied, about the completeness, accuracy, reliability, suitability or availability with respect to the book or the information, products, services, or related graphics contained in the book for any purpose. Any reliance you place on such information is therefore strictly at your own risk.

In no event will the author or publisher be liable for any loss or damage including without limitation, indirect or consequential loss or damage, or any loss or damage whatsoever arising from loss of data or profits arising out of, or in connection with, the use of this book.

The information contained in this book is not intended to be a substitute for professional advice. The reader should always seek the advice of a qualified professional before taking any action based on the information contained in this book.

The author and publisher do not assume any responsibility for errors or omissions in the book, nor do they assume any liability for any loss or damage caused by any reliance on the information contained in this book. The reader should independently verify any information before relying on it.

INTRODUCTION

Dear readers,

As a certified public accountant with years of experience helping individuals navigate the complex world of taxes, I am thrilled to introduce my latest book, *"The Savvy Taxpayer Playbook: Winning Strategies for Beating the IRS at Their Own Game"*. This book is designed to provide a comprehensive overview of the US tax system and offer practical advice for maximizing deductions, reducing taxes, and achieving financial freedom.

The US tax system can be overwhelming and confusing, and many individuals struggle to understand their tax obligations and make the most of their tax situation. That's why I wrote this book - to help individuals like you gain a deeper understanding of taxes and learn how to take control of your finances.

This book is written for individuals of all ages and levels of financial knowledge, from recent graduates to seasoned professionals. Whether you are just starting to think about your financial future or are already well on your way to retirement, this book is for you.

In this book, I aim to pass on my knowledge and expertise in the field of taxes, including an overview of the US tax system, the types of income and deductions, how to calculate your tax liability, and how to plan for tax-efficient investing. I also cover important topics such as maximizing tax credits, and understanding tax forms and deadlines.

My goal with this book is to empower individuals to take control of their finances and make informed decisions about their taxes. I want to provide the tools and resources you need to achieve your financial goals and live the life you want.

By the end of this book, you can expect to have a solid understanding of the US tax system, be able to calculate your tax liability with confidence, and have a plan for maximizing your deductions and reducing your taxes. You will have a roadmap for achieving financial freedom and will be well on your way to reaching your financial goals.

This book was written basically for individual taxpayers. If you are a small business owner, then check out my earlier book: *The Small Business Owner's Tax-Saving Bible: Insider Tips and Loopholes to Avoid IRS Penalties and Maximize Savings*

So let's dive in! Whether you are a seasoned tax expert or just starting to think about your financial future, I am confident that this book will provide you with the knowledge and guidance you need to make the most of your tax situation.

Sincerely,

Mack O'Hara
Certified Public Accountant

Chapter 1

Overview of the US tax system

"A fine is a tax for doing something wrong. A tax is a fine for doing something right!"

- Treasury Secretary PAUL O'NEILL, March 20, 2002

The United States tax system is a complex and multi-faceted system that is designed to generate revenue for the federal government. The system is based on the idea of progressive taxation, which means that individuals and businesses are taxed at different rates based on their income. The US tax system includes several different types of taxes, including federal income tax, state income tax, and payroll taxes.

Federal income tax is a tax on individuals' and businesses' income and is the largest source of revenue for the federal government. The tax is calculated based on taxable income, which is the amount of income that is subject to taxation after deductions and exemptions have been taken into account. The tax rate for individuals is determined by their taxable income, with higher earners paying a higher tax rate.

State income tax is a tax on individuals' and businesses' income that is levied by individual states. The tax rate and rules for state income tax vary from state to state, but it is generally calculated based on taxable income.

Payroll taxes are taxes that are deducted from an individual's salary or wages and are used to fund Social Security and Medicare. The taxes are split between the employer and the employee, with each contributing a portion of the total tax owed.

In addition to these types of taxes, the US tax system also includes various deductions and credits, such as those for charitable contributions, education expenses, and home office expenses. These deductions and credits can reduce an individual's taxable income, resulting in lower tax liability.

When the present income tax legislation was adopted in 1913, only one out of every 271 Americans was impacted; the vast majority of Americans' taxable earnings did not exceed the exempt level of $3,000 for individuals and $4,000 for couples. Those who had been affected pay a rate of 1% on taxable income up to $20,000 and a maximum of 6% on income over that level. In 1916, the average tax rate was 2.75 percent for the 437,036 individual tax returns submitted. In fiscal 2013, 146 million individual income tax returns were submitted, and the IRS processed over two billion pieces of paper—enough to span over 200 miles if laid side by side.

You pay too much in taxes, and it costs you too much to file your returns. Here are a few "for example:"

◆ *Even after correcting for inflation, the United States received twice as much money from income taxes in 2001 as it did in 1981.*

◆ *The burden on the public of complying with the tax system increased by 250 million hours in 2000, resulting in an overall rise of 180 million hours in the burden on the public of federal agencies' collection of information.*

Let us now discuss intricacy. By 2009, our tax regulations required 70,320 pages and 3.7 million words. It is already almost 4 million words long. The epic book War and Peace is 1,444 pages long and has 660,000 words, while the Bible is 1,291 pages long and contains 774,746 words.

◆ *The documentation received by the IRS would circle the globe 36 times, according to Daniel J. Mitchell of the Heritage Foundation.*

◆ *Every year, the IRS sends approximately 10,000,000 correction notifications. 5,000,000 of them are incorrect!*

◆ *The IRS has lost over 6,400 computer tapes and cartridges.*

◆ *In 1948, the average American household with children paid 3% in income and payroll taxes to the federal government.*

Time is money, and these dollars sap your capacity to save and invest, while inflation exacerbates your financial issues by eroding your ability to merely keep up.

You lose even if your earnings stay at pace with inflation. For example, suppose you had a taxable income of $89,350 in 2014 and pay $18,194 in taxes. You still have $71,156 to spend. With inflation and an 8% rise, you would now make $96,635 and pay $20,234 in taxes, leaving you with $76,401 to spend. However, owing to inflation, this $76,401 is now only worth $70,289. The progressive nature of your tax system, along with the purchasing power decay induced by inflation, has reduced your actual purchasing power by $71,156 - $70,289 = $867 on a $7,285 rise in wages! The impact of state and social security taxes exacerbates your financial situation.

What are your options? One easy solution is to try to decrease your taxes, and the rest of this book will show you how. Some of the approaches in this book are the result of combining complex and intricate tax law parts, yet they are all perfectly legal. Some are lawful not because Congress wanted them to be, but because both Congress and the Internal Revenue Service were negligent in their research and the tax code wording enabling them exists.

While Congress creates tax legislation, the courts read and interpret it. The IRS and the courts frequently disagree in their readings of various code parts and their applications—the courts invariably win. Even if a tax consequence contradicts original congressional purpose, the courts must and do uphold the code's text. Such consequences are the law, and they may only be amended or abolished by congressional action. Until such action is taken, the American taxpayer has every legal right to employ such code combinations to cut, lessen, or even totally eliminate taxes.

Individuals must pay taxes, but not more than the law requires. You've chosen the wrong book though if you wish to make voluntary donations to our federal Treasury.

On the other hand, Congress intended most of the tactics described here. In many circumstances, legitimately minimizing your income tax obligation benefits both you and America. Certain types of receipts are purposefully omitted from gross income for tax purposes in order to accomplish a certain economic or social goal. These measures, which are sometimes referred to as "tax breaks," are especially designed to stimulate certain sorts of activities.

Tax breaks have the same impact on the federal budget as direct spending since they reflect income that the federal government does not receive. These unique tax provisions, therefore, have been designated "tax expenditures" or "tax aids" by the Treasury Department.

These expenditures are revenue losses caused by tax code provisions that provide special or selective tax relief to particular categories of taxpayers. These laws either promote or offer particular assistance to specific taxpayers. The federal government, for example, aims to encourage particular types of investment. Thus, accelerated rather than straight-line depreciation encourages corporate investment. This tax break has been enacted in order for businesses to have more cash to expand. Tax breaks aid in the creation of new enterprises and jobs.

Having more employment generate more paychecks, and the increased wages generate more taxes. Everyone gains in the long run if everything functions as it should.

Other tax expenditure rules, on the other hand, have been implemented as "relief provisions" to alleviate "tax burdens" or "simplify tax computations." The aged and the blind, for example, receive extra financial benefits through a deduction known as the "additional amount." The retirement income credit and the possible exclusion of social security annuity payments from taxable income are further examples of "personal or tax hardship" advantages for the elderly.

These revenue losses are known as tax "expenditures" because they are payments or expenditures made by the federal government through tax cuts rather than direct grants. A remission of tax liability is similar to a payment in the same way that debt forgiveness is equivalent to a payment.

According to the Congressional Budget Office, 92 provisions were classified as tax expenditures in 1980. Based on legislation in existence at the start of 1980, these were anticipated to cost $206 billion in fiscal year 1981. However, it's important to note that individual tax expenditures can change from year to year based on a variety of factors, including changes in tax laws, economic conditions, and inflation. It's always a good idea to consult with a tax professional or use up-to-date tax software to get an accurate estimate of your individual tax expenditures.

The financial advantages provided by tax expenditure provisions are similar to those provided by entitlement programs on the spending side of the budget. A tax expenditure provision can give further tax relief in the following ways:

◆ *Special exclusions, exemptions, and deductions that reduce taxable income and hence result in a lower tax payment, such as tax-exempt municipal bond interest or the exclusion of employee discounts or dependent care assistance programs from taxable income.*

◆ *Preferential rates, which minimize obligations by applying lower rates to all or a portion of a taxpayer's income, such as the special lowered maximum tax rate on long-term capital gains income.*

◆ *Special credits, such as the child tax credit or the foreign tax credit, that are deducted from the tax liability rather than the income on which the taxes are calculated.*

◆ *Tax deferrals, which often come from allowing deductions that are correctly traceable to a future year (for example, accelerated depreciation allowances) under conventional accounting principles: By paying later rather than now, the taxpayer effectively obtains an interest-free loan of the deferred burden.*

Alternative means of giving federal subsidies include taxation and direct expenditure. Almost any tax expenditure can be recast as a spending program, and the majority of spending programs may be substituted by tax expenditures. Thus, the option between taxation and direct expenditure is fundamentally one of various administrative procedures. Once it is determined that a specific subsidy is worthwhile, the question of how to provide that subsidy emerges. However, the following criteria have been considered while creating or evaluating any subsidy program:

◆ *Price and efficiency. What is the cost of the program? How properly targeted is the program—that is, does it reach just people who it is designed to reach? Does it give the motivation or advantage that it was intended to provide? Does it achieve its aim at the lowest possible cost?*
◆ *Justice and equity. Is the subsidy benefit spread fairly?*
◆ *Administration simplicity. How much does it cost to run the program? How soon will the benefits be distributed? Can the benefits be provided just to those who are eligible for them?*
◆ *Budget transparency and control. Is the Congress required to examine each program on a regular basis? Are its expenses susceptible to congressional oversight?*

However, many of these expenditures are the product of special interest organizations demanding relief provisions for their own constituents.

Why, for example, is there a separate "standard deduction" amount for the blind but not for the deaf? The solution, I believe, may have more to do with the two groups' political and lobbying might than with any intrinsic difference in the problems. These particular provisions are also a result of the political demands of our specific members of Congress. These are non-budgetary expenditures that seem as a decrease in revenues rather than an increase in legislative spending. In effect, they allow our legislators to expand our federal fiscal imbalance and spend more tax dollars without making it appear that they are doing so.

Arguments are made that tax breaks are straightforward and require significantly less government oversight and complexity than direct expenditures. It has also been suggested that these incentives boost private sector participation in social initiatives and favor private decision making over government-centered decision making.

The topic of this book is not whether the stated benefits of tax breaks are real or if their flaws exceed their purported benefits. The fact that they exist is significant. To reduce or eliminate your taxes entirely, you must first acknowledge that the tactics described in this book are both legal and, for the most part, deliberately intended by Congress. It is hardly surprising that the Internal Revenue Service has not made them generally known. Despite public statements and repeated denials, the Internal Revenue Service is a revenue collector. While the stated purpose is to administer the law fairly, the service's mission is to collect your tax money. No Internal Revenue agent has ever gotten or will ever receive a raise or promotion for advising a taxpayer on how to arrange their financial condition in order to decrease or eliminate taxes.

You may either spend thousands of dollars to a professional tax practitioner, attorney, or accountant to learn such tactics, or you can skip through to the next chapter.

Chapter 2

Tax Structure

Like the old tax system, our present tax system requires taxpayers to calculate their own taxes. It also requires each taxpayer to file a tax return and pay any taxes owed to the government by specific dates. Failure to complete these standards may result in fines, penalties, and, in severe situations, jail time. Furthermore, the Internal Revenue Service (IRS) assesses interest on unpaid taxes.

Many people seek the assistance of tax specialists, who prepare almost half of all tax returns submitted. Despite the fact that many taxpayers engage tax specialists to file their tax forms, every taxpayer should have a fundamental awareness of tax regulations. This knowledge will assist them in preparing their own taxes or anticipating the information tax specialists would want to prepare their customers' returns.

This fundamental information will also assist them in reviewing a professionally prepared return before filing it with the IRS. Finally, understanding the tax rules can assist taxpayers in identifying possible difficulties before taxable events occur. Taxpayers can lower their tax liability by preparing ahead of time. The first section of this chapter presents an overview of the existing income tax structure in the United States. The final section provides basic tax planning principles.

Goals of Income Taxation

The federal income tax system produces funds (tax revenues) to assist the government in meeting its annual running expenditures. The United States Constitution grants Congress the authority to adopt and amend federal tax laws. As a result, it is up to Congress to decide how much to tax and at what rate to raise money. However, Congress utilizes tax legislation to achieve a variety of economic, political, and social objectives. Redistributing the country's wealth, supporting economic development and full employment, and changing certain attitudes are among them.

If the government's purpose is to promote employment, for example, Congress can decrease taxes and give citizens more money to spend. Increased taxpayer expenditure would raise demand for goods and services, necessitating the hiring of additional people to manufacture the goods and supply the services. The excise tax applied to the cost of cigarettes is an example of Congress using tax legislation to discourage specific behavior. With an extra expense, the expected outcome is a decrease in cigarette demand.

Basic Tax Formula

Taxes are levied by governments by applying a tax rate to a tax base. The tax base in the income tax system is taxable income. Simply expressed, *"taxable income"* is the difference between the amount of income taxed by the government and the deductions allowed from that income.

Income is typically defined as anything that enables wealth to rise. Not all products that improve one's wealth, however, are taxed. Gross income is money that is taxed by the government.

The majority of deductions are costs that the government authorizes to be deducted from gross income. Some deductions, however, are unrelated to expenses.

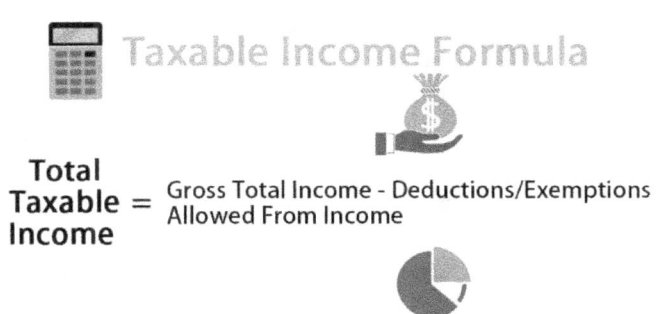

Figure 1-1: Taxable Income Formula

A *"taxpayer"* is defined in this book as any individual or company obligated to submit an income tax return with the Internal Revenue Service (IRS). Regular companies (sometimes known as "C corporations") are commercial entities that pay tax on their taxable income each year. They are equivalent to individual taxpayers in this way. However, not everyone pays income taxes. The IRS requires flow-through companies to declare their gross revenue and tax deductions. However, the owners of these entities are responsible for paying taxes on their individual portions of the entity's taxable revenue. Flow-through entities include partnerships and S companies.

Although the focus of this book is on the individual taxpayer, businesses are occasionally referenced. However, unique restrictions may apply solely to a certain set of taxpayers. The basic method for calculating taxable income, for example, is the same for businesses and individuals. Individuals, on the other hand, are eligible to additional forms of deductions and consequently employ an extended taxable income calculation (descibed below).

For the purposes of this book, unless it is evident from the discussion that the phrase *"taxpayer"* refers to a specific type of taxpayer (such as an individual or a company), when the term *"taxpayer"* is used while discussing a tax law, that legislation applies to all sorts of taxpayers.

Calculation of Taxes Owed (To Be Refunded)
Taxable income × Tax rate = Income tax liability + Additional taxes − Tax credits = **Final tax due (refund)**

Deductions VS. Credits

The distinction between a deduction and a credit is important. Tax credits reduce tax liability. Tax deductions reduce taxable income. Tax credits reduce the taxpayer's taxes by the amount of the tax credit. Deductions reduce the taxpayer's taxes by the amount of the deduction times the taxpayer's tax rate.

For example, a $100 deduction reduces taxable income by $100. This saves $15 in taxes if the tax rate is 15% ($100 × 15%), but saves $35 if the tax rate is 35% ($100 × 35%).

A $100 tax credit, on the other hand, reduces taxes by $100 regardless of the taxpayer's tax rate.

Individual Taxpayers

Although many forms of revenue exist, the notion of gross income is the same for all taxpayers. In other words, the government taxes certain forms of income while not taxing others. Tax regulations also permit a number of deductions in calculating taxable income. Individuals can lower their taxable income through a combination of business and personal deductions. As a result, the tax laws divide the deductions available to people into two categories: deductions for AGI and deductions from AGI.

AGI deductions are more personal in nature. Individual taxpayers' tax rate on taxable income is determined by their filing status. A person's filing status is determined by whether or not he or she is married on the last day of the tax year, among other things. More information on the regulations for each filing status is provided later in the book.

(1) married filing jointly (MFJ); (2) married filing separately (MFS); (3) qualified widow(er); (4) head of household (HOH); and (5) single. are the five filing statuses.

Tax Formula for Individuals
Income from all sources − Exempt income = Gross income
− Deductions for AGI (adjusted gross income) = AGI
− Deductions from AGI
       Itemized deductions or standard deduction
       Exemption deduction (personal and dependency)
= Taxable income

× *Tax rate = Income tax liability + Additional taxes*
 − *Tax credits =* ***Final tax due (refund)***

Individuals who are obligated to file an income tax return must do so using one of the following forms:

1. Form 1040EZ, Income Tax Return for Singles and Joint Filers Who Do Not Have Dependents
2. Form 1040A, Individual Income Tax Return for the United States
3. Form 1040, United States Individual Income Tax Return

Form 1040EZ, as the name implies, is the simplest of the tax forms to complete. However, only some taxpayers are eligible to utilize Form 1040EZ. We will discuss more about tax forms in the coming chapters.

Gross Income

Taxpayers must be able to calculate their taxable income. The Internal Revenue Code (the Code) is the body of tax legislation enacted by Congress. The Code defines gross income as all money flowing to a taxpayer from whatever source. It then exempts some types of income from taxes.

The Code specifies the following gross revenue sources (and indicates the existence of others):

1. Service compensation, including salary, wages, fees, commissions, fringe benefits, and so on.
2. Gross business income
3. Gains from property disposal
4. Interest

5. *Rents*
6. *Dividends*
7. *Royalties*
8. *Separate maintenance payments and alimony*
9. *Pensions*
10.*Income from life insurance proceeds*
11 *Pensions*
12.*Debt forgiveness income*
13.*Distribution partnership income and a pro rata portion of S Corporation revenue*
14.*Income from a decedent's estate*
15.*Income from an estate or trust interest*

Taxpayers often review their many sources of income (stuff that improve their wealth) and deduct exempt income to establish gross income. Whatever the type or name of an income item, sufficient authorisation is required to exclude it from gross revenue. Such authority may be found in tax statutes such as the Code, Treasury Regulations, IRS rulings, or case law. To calculate taxable income, taxpayers subtract permitted deductions from gross income.

It is critical that taxpayers calculate their gross income accurately. When a taxpayer's gross income surpasses a specific threshold, he or she must file an income tax return. Tax penalties may apply if a valid return is not filed on time. In addition, if a taxpayer understates his or her gross income by more than 25%, the IRS is allowed longer time to examine the person's return. Finally, depending on the amount of the other person's gross income, persons may be granted or refused a deduction for claiming another person as a dependant.

Chapter 3

Deductions and Exemptions

Individual taxpayers can take advantage of two types of deductions: deductions for AGI and deductions from AGI. Taxpayers subtract deductions for AGI from gross income to arrive at AGI. They then subtract deductions from AGI to arrive at taxable income.

There are two kinds of AGI deductions. The larger of a taxpayer's itemized deductions or the standard deduction is used. The other is a deduction for (personal and dependent) exemptions. AGI is not calculated for corporations, partnerships, estates, or trusts.

Deductions for AGI

The AGI of a person is defined by the Code as gross income less specified deductions. Among the significant deductions are:
1. Deductions for trade and business for company owners
2. Losses on the sale of commercial or investment property
3. Deductions for rental and royalty income
4. Certain payments to self-employed people' retirement plans
5. Certain typical Individual Retirement Account contributions (IRAs)
Early withdrawal penalties on certificates of deposit
7. Paid alimony;

8. Qualified moving expenses
9. Half of the self-employment tax
10. Self-employed people's health insurance premiums
11. Contributions made by individuals to medical savings or health savings accounts
12. Interest on student loans.
13. Deduction for domestic manufacturing activities

Deductions from AGI

Individuals compute their AGI by subtracting the larger of their itemized deductions or their entire standard deduction. They then deduct their exemption deduction. In comparison to AGI deductions, itemized deductions are costs that are often more personal in nature. They include:

1. Medical expenses
2. Taxes
3. Interest
4. Charitable contributions
5. Casualty and theft losses
6. Employee business (job) expenses and some miscellaneous deductions
7. Other miscellaneous deductions

Standard Deduction

Individual taxpayers are qualified for standard deduction, which is a deduction from AGI. It is divided into two parts: the basic standard deduction and the additional standard deduction. Each year, both sums are increased for inflation. Taxpayers who file Forms 1040EZ or 1040A must take the standard deduction. In addition, when spouses file separate forms, both must itemize deductions or take the standard deduction. Thus, if one spouse itemizes, the standard deduction for the other spouse is $0. This compels the other spouse to do the same.

Basic Standard Deductions
The standard deduction amounts are divided into four categories. The amount that applies is determined on the filing status. A unique regulation applies to those claimed as dependents of another taxpayer (as discussed later in Standard Deduction for Dependents).

The standard deduction amounts for tax year 2021 (filed in 2022) are as follows:	
Filing Status	**Amount**
Married filing jointly (MFJ)	$25,100
Qualifying widow(er)	25,100
Head of household (HOH)	18,800
Single	12,550
Married filing separately (MFS)	12,550

Additional Standard Deduction
Blind and elderly taxpayers are entitled to an extra basic deduction. This extra deduction is only accessible to the taxpayer, which includes both spouses when filing a joint return. A taxpayer cannot claim an extra standard deduction for a dependant who is elderly or blind.

Three extra standard deduction amounts are available. Which amount is utilized is determined on the taxpayer's filing status

> **The additional standard deduction amounts for tax year 2021 (filed in 2022) are as follows:**
>
> | Filing Status | Amount |
> |---|---|
> | Married filing jointly (MFJ), Married filing separately (MFS), and Qualifying widow(er) | $1,300 |
> | Head of household (HOH) | $1,650 |
> | Single | $1,300 |
>
> **Note: The additional standard deduction is available to taxpayers who are age 65 or older, or who are blind. The amounts are adjusted annually**

To be eligible for an extra standard deduction, a taxpayer must be old or blind at the conclusion of the tax year (or at death). Individuals age the day before their calendar birthday for tax purposes, while the elderly are considered as having attained the age of 65. As a result, a taxpayer who turns 65 on January 1 is considered to be 65 for tax purposes as of December 31 of the prior year.

Blindness can be claimed as an extra deduction by failing a visual ability or field of vision test. With a corrective lens, vision in either eye cannot exceed 20/200 for the visual ability exam. The person's field of vision cannot exceed 20 degrees for the field of vision test. With a verified declaration from an eye doctor, the taxpayer supports the extra deduction for blindness.

Each case of old age and blindness has an extra deduction. Each spouse is entitled for both deductions in the case of married taxpayers. As a result, if both spouses are 65 years old, the total increased standard deduction is $2,600 (2 x $1,300).

If both spouses are over the age of 65 and one is blind, the additional deduction is $3,900 (3 x $1,300). The additional deduction for a single individual who is 65 and blind is $3,100 (2 x $1,550).

> Dani is 70 and blind. Her filing status is single. Dani's 2021 total standard deduction equals $15,210 ($12,550 + ($1,330 × 2)).
>
> Fred and Anna Kennedy are married and file a joint return (MFJ) in 2022. As of December 31, 2021, Fred is 70 and Anna is 64. Neither have any problems with their vision. The Kennedy's add to their $25,100 basic standard deduction for MFJ an additional $1,300 for Don's age. Their total standard deduction equals $26,400. If the Kennedy's itemized deductions exceed this amount, they will itemize. Otherwise they will subtract $26,400 from their AGI when computing their 2021 taxable income.

Standard Deductions for Dependents

A person who qualifies as a dependant of another taxpayer computes the basic standard deduction for tax year 2021 (filed in 2022) as follows:

(i) $1,100 or (ii) earned income + $350. The deduction cannot exceed the basic standard deduction for the filing status of the dependant. The basic standard deduction is increased by any additional standard deduction for which the dependant qualifies.

Married couples who file separate returns are subject to special requirements. If each spouse is claimed as a dependant by another taxpayer, the basic standard deduction for each spouse is restricted to the lesser of (i) $1,100 or (ii) the spouse's earned income plus $350. If one spouse itemizes deductions, the other spouse's total standard deduction is $0.

Earned income includes wages, tips, professional fees, and other money received for personal services given when calculating a dependent's basic standard deduction. It also includes taxable scholarships and self-employment net earnings.

> Deb, age 74, has no earned income and is claimed as a dependent on her son's tax return. Her 2021 basic standard deduction is limited to $1,100 (the greater of (i) $1,100 or (ii) $0 earned income + $350). Her additional standard deduction is $1,300. Sue deducts $2,400 ($1,100 + $1,300) from AGI when computing her 2014 taxable income.

Standard Deduction Worksheet for Dependents—Line 37   *Keep for Your Records*

Use this worksheet **only** if someone can claim you, or your spouse if filing jointly, as a dependent.

1. Add $250 to your **earned income***. Enter the total .... 1. _____
2. Minimum standard deduction 2. 750.00
3. Enter the **larger** of line 1 or line 2 .... 3. _____
4. Enter the amount shown below for your filing status.
   - Single or married filing separately—$4,750
   - Married filing jointly or qualifying widow(er)—$9,500   .... 4. _____
   - Head of household—$7,000
5. **Standard deduction.**
   a. Enter the **smaller** of line 3 or line 4. If born after January 1, 1939, and not blind, **stop here** and enter this amount on Form 1040, line 37. Otherwise, go to line 5b .... 5a. _____
   b. If born before January 2, 1939, or blind, multiply the number on Form 1040, line 36a, by $950 ($1,150 if single or head of household) .... 5b. _____
   c. Add lines 5a and 5b. Enter the total here and on Form 1040, line 37 .... 5c. _____

* **Earned income** includes wages, salaries, tips, professional fees, and other compensation received for personal services you performed. It also includes any amount received as a scholarship that you must include in your income. Generally, your earned income is the total of the amount(s) you reported on Form 1040, lines 7, 12, and 18, minus the amount, if any, on line 28

Figure 3-1: Standard Deduction Worksheet For Dependents

Exemptions

The personal exemption deduction was suspended for tax years 2018 through 2025 as part of the Tax Cuts and Jobs Act. As a result, there is no personal exemption deduction for tax year 2021 (filed in 2022).

It's important to note that the suspension of the personal exemption deduction is temporary and is set to expire after 2025. The future of the personal exemption deduction is subject to change based on legislative action.

The exemption amount, like the standard deduction amount, is updated for inflation each year. In general, the taxpayer may seek an exemption for himself or herself as well as anyone who qualifies as a dependant. Each spouse can claim a personal exemption if a married pair files a joint tax return. Exemptions are the largest tax deduction for many taxpayers. A married taxpayer with two dependent children, for example, decreases AGI by $15,800 (4 x $3,950).

Phase out exemptions
Before the suspension of the personal exemption deduction as part of the Tax Cuts and Jobs Act, the AGI phase-out range for the 2017 tax year (filed in 2018) was as follows:

Filing Status	Phase-Out Begins	Phase-Out Ends
Married filing jointly (MFJ) and qualifying widow(er)	$313,800	$436,300
Head of household (HOH)	$287,650	$410,150
Single	$261,500	$384,000
Married filing separately (MFS)	$156,900	$218,150

Table 3-1. AGI Phase-Out Range for the 2017 Exemption Deduction

In general, as your AGI increased within the phase-out range, the amount of your personal exemption deduction was gradually reduced. If your AGI was above the upper limit of the phase-out range, you couldn't claim the personal exemption deduction.

Using the worksheet below, Chris and Suzie Rock calculate their exemption deduction. The Rocks file a joint return and claim their four children as dependents. Their AGI for 2018 is $328,610, which falls in the $313,800–$436,300 phase-out range for MFJ taxpayers.

1. Is the amount on Form 1040, line 38, more than the amount on line 4 below for your filing status?...1. _____

   ☐ **No.** Stop. Multiply $3,950 by the total number of exemptions claimed on line 6d of Form 1040 and enter the result on Form 1040, line 42.

   ☐ **Yes.** Continue.
2. Multiply $3,950 by the total number of exemptions claimed on line 6d of Form 1040 ....2. _____
3. Enter the amount from Form 1040, line 38...3. _____
4. Enter the amount shown below for your filing status:
   • Married filing separately—$152,525
   • Single—$254,200 ....4. _____
   • Head of household—$279,850
   • Married filing jointly or Qualifying widow(er)—$305,050
5. Subtract line 4 from line 3. If the result is more than $122,500 ($61,250 if married filing separately), **stop here.** You cannot take a deduction for exemptions...5. _____
6. Divide line 5 by $2,500 ($1,250 if married filing separately). If the result is not a whole number, round it up to the next higher whole number (for example, increase .00004 to 1)......................6. _____
7. Multiply line 6 by 2% (.02) and enter the result as a decimal (rounded to at least three places).........7. _____
8. Multiply line 2 by line 7 ....8. _____
9. Deduction for exemptions. Subtract line 8 from line 2. Enter the result here and on Form 1040, line 42..9. _____

Figure 3-2: Personal and Dependency Exemption Worksheet

> The worksheet above is used to compute the reduced exemption deduction for taxpayers whose AGI falls between the amounts shown in the two columns of Table 3-1. If AGI is lower than the lesser amount, the taxpayer's deduction is $3,950 times the total number of exemptions claimed. If AGI exceeds the higher amount, the exemption deduction is $0.

Personal Exemptions

A taxpayer normally deducts a personal exemption for himself or herself. When a married couple files a joint tax return, they are given two exemptions. A person who is listed as a dependant on another taxpayer's return, on the other hand, cannot claim a personal exemption. The personal exemption amount is unaffected by the death of a taxpayer. On a decedent's last return, the entire exemption is permitted. No prorating is required.

Exemptions for Dependents

Each individual who qualifies as a "dependent" may be exempted by the taxpayer. While little children and elderly parents are often included on the taxpayer's list of dependents, others may be eligible. To claim an exemption, each dependent's social security number (SSN) must be included on the tax return. There will be no dependency exemption if you do not have an SSN.

A qualified kid, a qualifying relative, or a qualifying nonrelative may qualify as the taxpayer's dependant. The next sections go through the regulations for each of these three categories. A dependant must fulfill all of the standards for the relevant category. Even if the qualifying dependant files a tax return, the taxpayer may claim an exemption for them. The dependant, however, cannot claim a personal exemption on his or her own return. A complete exemption may also be claimed by the taxpayer for a dependant who was born or died during the year. A stillborn kid is not eligible for an exemption.

Qualifying Child

Those who satisfy the criteria for a qualifying kid are one category of people who may qualify as a dependant. The first requirement is that a qualified kid be younger than the taxpayer. A eligible youngster must also pass each of the six exams listed below.

1. Relationship test for qualifying child
2. Age test
3. Residency test
4. Support test for eligible children
5. Joint return test
6. Citizenship examination

Test of Relationship for Qualifying Child

Each of the following people meets the relationship requirements for a qualified child:

◆ *The taxpayer's natural child, stepchild, adopted child, eligible foster child, or descendants of any of these children (grandchildren, great-grandchildren, and so on). A kid placed with the taxpayer by an authorized agency or by a court order is considered as eligible foster child.*

◆ *Brothers and sisters of the taxpayer, half-brothers and half-sisters, stepbrothers and stepsisters, or offspring of these siblings (the taxpayer's nieces and nephews).*

> Denise's household includes her son, her son's daughter (Denise's granddaughter), her sister, her sister's son (Denise's nephew), her younger stepbrother, and her stepbrother's daughter (her stepniece). Each of these persons is younger than Denise and passes the relationship test with respect to Denise. Thus, if the other five tests are passed, these persons would qualify as Denise's dependents using the qualifying child rules.

Age Test

The age test does not apply to those who are fully and permanently incapacitated. A qualified kid must be under the age of 19, or a full-time student under the age of 24, for all others. A full-time student is someone who satisfies the institution's full-time enrollment criterion and attends classes for at least part of each of the year's five calendar months. The institution must have a full-time faculty, course offerings, and a regular student body. A eligible youngster who works full-time during the day and goes to night school cannot be a full-time student. Enrollment in correspondence or job training courses does not qualify a person for full-time status.

Test of Residency
A eligible kid must share the taxpayer's address for more than half of the year. Temporary absences are overlooked, such as those caused by sickness, education, business, or vacation. There are also particular restrictions for children of divorced or separated parents.

Support Test for a Qualifying Child
A qualified youngster cannot contribute more than half of his or her own support. Food, clothes, education, medical and dental treatment, entertainment, transportation, and accommodation are all examples of support. It excludes burial expenses and payments for life insurance premiums. Scholarships from educational institutions are also not considered support. Consider a child who earns a $4,500 college scholarship in a year when the taxpayer contributes $3,800 to the child's upkeep. Because the tax law disregards the $4,500, the taxpayer fulfills the support criteria to claim the kid as a dependant if no other sources of support exist. As a result, the taxpayer is considered to have given the entire $3,800 in child support.

Generally, the status and source of assistance funding have no bearing. Social security income, school loans, and welfare payments all count if the dependant spends them on necessities. The concept of support, however, excludes monies paid by the state for training and education of a disabled or mentally ill kid.

Joint Return Test

A married individual cannot submit a combined return to qualify as the dependant of another taxpayer. The IRS makes an exemption when a married couple's joint return is used only to seek a refund of all prepaid taxes for the year. When all three of the following requirements are satisfied, something occurs:

1. Neither spouse is obliged to submit a tax return
2. a separate return filed by either spouse would result in no tax obligation; and
3. the sole purpose to file a return is to get a refund of any federal income taxes withheld.

> Amy provides 75% of her married daughter's support. For the year, her daughter earns $3,100 working part-time. Amy's son-in-law receives $4,000 of nontaxable interest. The couple lives with Amy for over half of the year. To get a refund of the income taxes withheld from the daughter's wages, the couple files a joint return. Because their combined gross income is only $3,100, the tax law does not require them to file a tax return. Also, both the daughter and son-in-law would have a zero tax liability if they filed separate tax returns. Thus, both the daughter and son-in-law pass the joint return test.

Citizenship Test

A dependant must be an American citizen or a resident of Canada or Mexico. An exemption exists, however, for foreign-born children adopted by US residents residing overseas. These children may be considered dependents if they live with the taxpayer for the whole year.

Children of Divorced or Separated Parents

When a couple divorces or splits, one parent may claim an exemption for a kid (son or daughter) who meets all of the requirements for a qualifying child if the parents share custody of the child for more than half the year. The tax legislation exempts the parent with the longest real custody (custodial parent). The exception may, however, be granted to the noncustodial parent by the custodial parent. This is accomplished by having the custodial parent fill up and sign Form 8332 (or a similar declaration), which is then given to the noncustodial parent. The release might span one or more years.

The noncustodial parent must attach the release statement to his or her tax return for each year it is in force.

Form **8332** (Rev. January 2010) Department of the Treasury Internal Revenue Service

Release/Revocation of Release of Claim to Exemption for Child by Custodial Parent

▶ Attach a separate form for each child.

OMB No. 1545-0074 Attachment Sequence No. **115**

Name of noncustodial parent | **Noncustodial parent's social security number (SSN)** ▶

Part I **Release of Claim to Exemption for Current Year**

I agree not to claim an exemption for ______________ Name of child

for the tax year 20___.

Signature of custodial parent releasing claim to exemption | Custodial parent's SSN | Date

Note. If you choose not to claim an exemption for this child for future tax years, also complete Part II.

Part II **Release of Claim to Exemption for Future Years** (If completed, see **Noncustodial Parent** on page 2.)

I agree not to claim an exemption for ______________ Name of child

for the tax year(s)______________ (Specify. See instructions.)

Signature of custodial parent releasing claim to exemption | Custodial parent's SSN | Date

Part III **Revocation of Release of Claim to Exemption for Future Year(s)**

I revoke the release of claim to an exemption for ______________ Name of child

for the tax year(s)______________ (Specify. See instructions.)

Signature of custodial parent revoking the release of claim to exemption | Custodial parent's SSN | Date

Figure 2-3: Form 8332

By completing and signing Part II of Form 8332, the custodial parent, has agreed to allow the other parent to claim their child as a dependent for the certain tax years.

Part I of Form 8332 is completed if the custodial parent wants to give away the dependency exemption for only one year. Part III is completed if the custodial parent wants to revoke a previously granted right given to the noncustodial parent to claim the child as a dependent. For all years in which a revocation is in effect, Form 8332 is attached to the custodial parent's tax return.

Rules for Claiming a Dependency Exemption in the Event of a Tie

When numerous taxpayers are eligible to claim a qualified kid as a dependant, only one of them may do so. Typically, the eligible parties may agree on who will claim the qualifying kid. When one of the eligible individuals is the kid's parent, however, a non-parent can only claim the qualifying child if the AGI of the non-parent's is greater than the AGI of the parent. If the parties cannot agree on who will claim the eligible kid, the Code offers the "tie-break" criteria outlined below.

◆ *When just one of the kid's parents is among those who can claim the child as a dependant, the dependency exemption is granted to the parent.*

◆ *When both parents meet the requirements to claim the child as a dependant, the exemption is granted to the custodial parent (or the noncustodial parent if the custodial parent has signed over the dependency exemption to the noncustodial parent, as indicated above).*

◆ *When both parents meet the requirements to claim the kid as a dependant and the child spends equal amounts of time with each parent (there is no custodial parent), the exemption is awarded to the one with the highest AGI.*

◆ *When neither parent is qualified to claim the kid as a dependant, the dependency exemption is awarded to the (non-parent) eligible individual with the greatest AGI.*

> Diane and her son, Dave, live with Diane's father. Diane's AGI is $20,000; her father's AGI is $60,000. Jeffrey is a qualifying child to both Diane and her father. If Diane and her father cannot agree on who gets to claim Dave as a qualifying child, under the tie-break rules, Diane (the parent) gets to claim Jeffrey as her dependent.

Qualifying Relative

Qualifying relatives of the taxpayer are a second category of people who can be claimed as a dependant. Anyone who satisfies the following five criteria but does not meet the qualifications to be a qualified kid is considered a qualifying relative.

1. Relationship test for qualifying relatives
2. Support test for qualifying relatives
3. Gross income test
4. Joint return test
5. Citizenship test

The combined return and citizenship exams follow the same procedures as a qualified kid. The remaining three tests are covered in the sections that follow.

Relationship test for qualifying relatives

The relationship test for qualifying relatives requires the individual to be a taxpayer's relative. To qualify as a dependant, a relative does not have to reside with the taxpayer. The following individuals qualify as a taxpayer's relatives for income tax purposes, according to the Code.

◆ *Half-brother, half-sister, stepbrother, or stepsister*

◆ *A taxpayer's child, grandchild, or other descendant, including a lawfully adopted child*

◆ *The taxpayer's stepchild, but not the stepchild's descendants*

◆ *Parent, grandparent, or other ancestor (but not a foster parent, foster grandparent, etc.)*

◆ *Stepparent*

◆ *Father-In-law, mother-in-law, son-in-law, daughter-in-law, brother-in-law, or sister-in-law,*

◆ *a nephew or a niece (but only if related by blood, not by marriage)*

◆ *Aunt or uncle (but only if related by blood, not by marriage)*

The tax legislation establishes permanent legal connections with in-laws at the moment of a couple's marriage that remain after the couple divorces or a spouse dies. As a result, following his wife's death, a husband may claim an exemption for his mother-in-law (provided the other four tests for qualifying relatives are met). Aunts, uncles, nieces, and nephews are only considered relatives if they are related to the taxpayer by blood (not through marriage). Relatives of either spouse may qualify as dependents on a combined return. Even though one's spouse's aunt does not qualify as a relative, on a combined return, the aunt is a related of the spouse and may qualify as the couple's dependant.

Support test for qualifying relatives
The support test for a qualified relative differs from the support test for a qualifying kid. For a qualifying relative to pass the support test, the taxpayer usually must provide more than 50% of the person's total support during the tax year. Support from either spouse counts on a combined return.

Food, clothes, education, medical and dental treatment, entertainment, transportation, and accommodation are all examples of assistance. When a taxpayer provides housing for a relative, the IRS considers the fair rental value of the room to be support. The rent a taxpayer may expect to earn from a stranger for the same dwelling is considered fair rental value. A reasonable rental price includes the use of one room or a proportionate piece of a property. When given to (or purchased for) a relative, capital items such as vehicles and furnishings count as support. Support also covers wedding expenses paid for a relative. Scholarships from educational institutions are not considered assistance, and the status and source of support monies often make no difference. Payments for life insurance premiums and burial expenses are also not considered assistance. These are the same standards that apply to determining assistance for an eligible kid.

To assess whether a taxpayer contributes more than half of a relative's support, the taxpayer computes the relative's total support, which is comprised of three amounts:

1. The fair rental value of the relative's lodging.

2. The unrelated relative's part of household expenditures (such as food but not housing).

3. Other support-related costs directly spent or paid to or for the relative.

Multiple Support Agreements

A group of persons (e.g., children) may give support for a dependant (e.g., parent), but no one person (including the dependent) contributes more than 50% of the assistance. A unique rule permits one group member to seek the exemption. The member of the group seeking the exemption may change from year to year. To qualify for the exemption, the group member must: 1. provide more than 10% of the dependent's support, 2. provide more than 50% of the dependent's support with the other group members, and 3. be able to claim the person as a dependant elsewhere.

Furthermore, the group must agree on who will receive the exception.

It is not commonplace for the exemption to be rotated among group members from year to year. Once the group has reached the following agreement:

1. Group members who do not claim the exemption must sign a declaration relinquishing their right to claim the exemption and return it to the claiming member. The following information must be included in the statement: (a) the applicable tax year, (b) the name of the dependant, and (c) the name,

address, and social security number of the individual waiving the exemption. The claiming member then keeps this declaration as proof of exemption. It is not submitted along with the tax return.

2. The claiming member files Form 2120, Multiple Support Declaration, along with his or her tax return. This form includes all eligible individuals who have waived their right to claim an exemption for the dependant in issue.

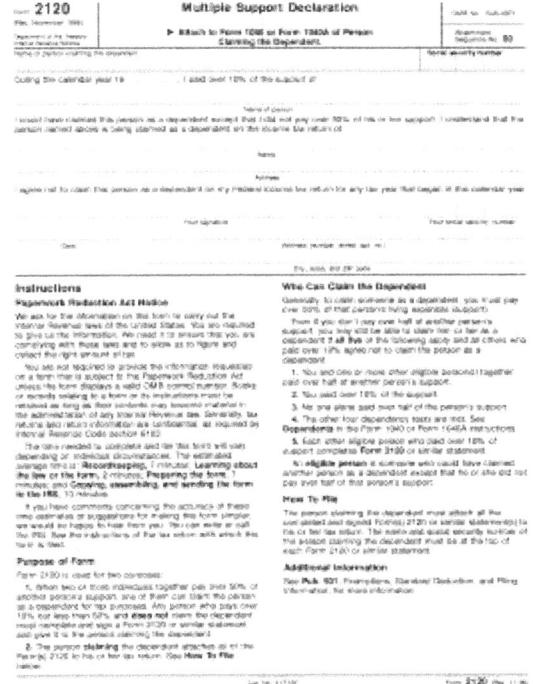

Figure 2-4: Form 2120. Multiple Support Declaration.

Gross Income Test

The gross income test for the dependency exemption is still used in current tax law. However, the exemption amount has been suspended for tax years 2018 through 2025 as part of the Tax Cuts and Jobs Act.

In addition, gross income includes a wide variety of income sources, including but not limited to wages, salaries, tips, taxable interest, dividends, capital gains, rental income, business income, and any other income that is subject to tax. It's important to note that gross income does not include nontaxable income, such as gifts, inheritances, life insurance proceeds, and certain other types of income that are not subject to taxation. The exact definition of gross income may vary depending on the specific tax law and rules applicable to a particular tax year

Qualifying Non-relatives

A person who is unrelated to the taxpayer may qualify as the taxpayer's dependant. To qualify, a non-relative must fulfill the same requirements as relatives.

1. Citizenship test
2. Support test
3. Gross income test
4. Joint return test

Furthermore, the individual must live with the taxpayer for the whole year. The death or birth of these people will reduce the "entire year" requirement to the time they were alive.

Temporary absences for sickness, school, vacation, employment, or military duty are also included as time spent with the taxpayer. Indefinite nursing home stays for continuous medical treatment may be regarded as transitory.

Filing Status

Anyone who submits a return falls into one of five filing status categories. In some circumstances, the taxpayer's filing status dictates which tax return he or she must submit. The filing status also impacts the standard deduction amount used in calculating taxable income, as well as the tax rates utilized in calculating tax liabilities.

In general, married couples have two filing options: **married filing jointly** or **married filing separately**. In some circumstances, married taxpayers can claim head of household status. Unmarried people can file under the **qualified widow(er), head of household, or single status.** The most advantageous tax rates are shared by married filing jointly and qualified widow(er), followed by head of household and finally single.
The least advantageous tax rates apply to taxpayers who file **married filing separately**. Taxpayers would like to qualify for the lowest feasible tax rate based on their marital status whenever possible.

Married Filing Jointly.
The marital status of a taxpayer is decided for tax purposes on the final day of the tax year. As a result, if a person is married on the last day of the tax year, he or she may submit a joint return with his or her spouse. Similarly, if you are formally divorced or

separated before the end of the year, you cannot file a joint return. If the divorce or legal separation has not been finalized by the end of the year, the pair is still legally married for tax purposes and may file a joint return.

Even if only one spouse has income, a married couple can file a joint return. A jointly filed tax return must be signed by both couples, making each spouse accountable for the total tax burden. If the marriage divorces, the IRS retains the power to collect any taxes due by either spouse.

> The Defense of Marriage Act (DOMA) is a federal law enacted in 1996. One part of DOMA defined marriage as a legal union between a man and a woman. For this reason, the IRS (a federal agency) did not recognize legal unions between same-sex couples. Hence, same-sex spouses were treated as unmarried taxpayers under federal tax law. In December 2012, the Supreme Court ruled that this part of DOMA was unconstitutional. Accordingly, spouses legally married in a state that recognizes same-sex marriages are treated as married taxpayers. It does not matter whether the state the couple lives in is one that recognizes same-sex marriage.

Year of Death
If a spouse dies, the date of death is also used to determine marital status. A final income tax return must be submitted on behalf of the decedent under tax law. In the year the spouse dies, a widow(er) may submit a combined return with the departed spouse. When the widow(er) files a joint return, she is entitled two personal exemptions in the year of death. Across the top of the return, the surviving spouse should write the term deceased, the name of the departed spouse, and the date of death. The

survivor should enter filing as surviving spouse on the spouse's signature line when signing the return. When someone other than the widow(er) is the deceased's personal representative, that person's signature, together with the phrase personal representative, shall appear in the deceased's signature line.

If a widow or widower remarries before the end of the year, she or he may file a joint return with the new spouse. Even if the survivor's new spouse files as married filing separately, a remarried widow(er) cannot file a joint return with the deceased spouse.

Married Filing Separately.
When both couples earn money, filing separate returns allows them to pay less taxes as a pair. Taxpayers should calculate their tax liabilities using both the combined and separate return statuses to see which one results in the lowest tax liability.

A number of variables may conspire against filing separate returns. Several tax benefits, such as the child and dependent care credit, education credits, and the earned income credit, are not accessible to married filing separately individuals.

Filing Separate Returns in Community Property States
The laws of the taxpayer's home state govern whether property is deemed common or separate property. As of 2023, there are nine community property states in the United States: Arizona, California, Idaho, Louisiana, Nevada, New Mexico, Texas, Washington, and Wisconsin. In these states, any property obtained during a marriage is

generally considered jointly-owned property, regardless of which spouse legally owns the property.

Community property laws can be complicated and differ from state to state. In general, community property laws apply to any property that is acquired during a marriage, including income, assets, and debts. However, there are some exceptions, such as gifts and inheritances, which may be considered separate property.

It's important to note that community property laws can have a significant impact on how assets are divided in the event of a divorce or the death of a spouse. Therefore, it's important for individuals who live in community property states to understand these laws and how they apply to their specific situation.

Election to File Joint or Separate Return
A decision to file a combined or separate return in one year does not transfer over to the following year. Each year stands on its own. After filing a combined return, a couple cannot switch to separate returns after the tax return's due date. Spouses who file separately may, however, shift to a combined return after the due date has passed. Within three years, an updated return must be submitted.

Qualifying Widow(er)
The survivor may be eligible for special status as a qualified widow(er) for two tax years following the death of a spouse. When filing as a qualified widow(er), the tax burden is calculated using the married filing jointly tax rates. They also take the

basic and extra standard deductions for married couples filing jointly. It is crucial to remember that, while qualified widows and widowers use the joint return tax rates and other amounts, they do not file a joint return. As a result, an eligible widow(er) can claim just one personal exemption.

A spouse who remarries does not qualify for qualifying widow(er) status. When a widow(er) remarries, she must file a joint or separate return with the new husband. To qualify for qualifying widow(er) status, a widow(er) must pay more than half of the household expenditures for the whole year in which the widow(er) and a dependent son or daughter dwell. This kid may be a qualifying foster, adoptive, natural, or stepchild of the taxpayer. Temporary absences from the household have no bearing on eligibility to register as an eligible widow (er). As a result, a son or daughter who attends a boarding school and goes home for vacation times is still considered a part of the widow(er)'s family. Hospital stays are treated the same way.

> Jack maintains a household where he and his 12-year-old dependent daughter live. Jack's wife died in 2020. Jack filed a joint return in 2020. Assuming Jack does not remarry and continues to claim his daughter as a dependent, he files his tax returns for 2021 and 2022 using qualifying widow(er) filing status.

Head of Household

Certain unmarried people can claim head of household status. The tax rates for heads of households are lower than those for single taxpayers, but higher than those for married couples filing jointly. Head of household position does not apply to taxpayers who may file as an eligible widow(er), since these individuals should utilize the more advantageous filing status.

To qualify for head of household status, the taxpayer must contribute more than half of the expense of sustaining a household in which a "qualifying child" or a relative or non-relative claimed as a dependent resides with the taxpayer for more than half of the year.

A dependent parent is not required to reside with the taxpayer. However, the taxpayer must pay more than half of the parent's annual household expenditures. Also,

1. A married "qualifying child" or a married child who is not a qualifying kid must pass each of the five dependence standards for a "qualified relative".

2. When a dependent child is utilized to achieve head of household status, custodial parents do not lose head of household status if they forgo their kid's right to be claimed as a dependent.

3. If the dependence exemption is secured through a multiple support arrangement, the head of household position is not possible.

Maintaining a household entails the taxpayer paying more than half of the annual household expenditures, which often include contributions for the mutual benefit of household inhabitants. These expenses include money spent on meals, utilities, and repairs. They exclude the value of services rendered by taxpayers or household members.

Candy is single and maintains a household where she and her 25-year-old unmarried son live. Candy provides all of her son's support during the year. The son is a full-time student and has no gross income. Because of his age, the son is not a qualifying child. He does, however, pass all five tests for a qualifying relative. Thus, Candy claims her son as a dependent and files as head of household.

Dan and Bruno divorced in 2010. Together they share custody of their 9-year-old son, Mark, for more than six months of the year and provide over half of his support. Dan has custody of Mark; however, he has waived his right to claim Mark as a dependent. Even though Bruno is entitled to the dependency exemption for Dan, for purposes of filing as head of household, Mark is a qualifying child for Dan, but not for Bruno. Thus, Dan files as head of household. Bruno's filing status is single.

Pat's husband died in 2013. Pat maintains a household where she lives with her married son and his wife. Neither the son nor the daughter-in-law qualifies as Pat's dependent. Pat also pays over half of the costs to maintain a separate home for her aging mother, who qualifies as Pat's dependent. Pat files as head of household because she maintains a household for her dependent mother. A dependent parent is the only person who can qualify Pat for head of household filing status without having to live with her.

Abandoned Spouses (Married Persons Who Live Apart)

Married people who do not reside with their spouses for the final six months of the year may be considered abandoned spouses. Abandoned spouses are classified as unmarried for tax reasons and hence qualify for head of household filing status.

A married taxpayer must complete these five requirements to qualify as an abandoned spouse.

1. No joint return is filed by the taxpayer.
2. The taxpayer lives with a son or daughter who is the taxpayer's natural, step, adopted, or eligible foster child for more than six months of the year.
3. During the year, the taxpayer pays more than half of the costs of house maintenance.
4. The taxpayer has at least one son or daughter who qualifies as a dependant. This regulation does not apply if the taxpayer meets all of the exemption requirements but has decided to provide the exemption to the noncustodial parent.
5. During the last six months of the tax year, the taxpayer did not live with his or her spouse at any time.

Amir and Naya Idrissa are legally separated. They have not lived together since March, 2020. In 2020, Naya pays more than half of the costs to maintain the home where she and her two children live. However, Naya has agreed to allow Jim to claim the children as dependents. As of the end of 2020, the Idrissas' divorce had not been finalized. Even though Naya cannot claim the children as dependents, she qualifies as an abandoned spouse. Her filing status for 2020 is head of household. Amir will claim the two children as his dependents, but he must file as married filing separately.

Single

Unmarried taxpayers who do not qualify as qualified widow(er) or head of household must file as single taxpayers. Unless head of household filing status exists, a person who is legally separated but not yet divorced files as a single taxpayer. Similarly, in the years after the death of a spouse, a widow(er) who has not remarried files as a single taxpayer unless the conditions for qualifying widow(er) or head of household are satisfied.

Individual Filing Requirements

Individuals who satisfy specific qualifications must file an income tax return under our self-reporting tax system. Current filing requirements are mostly determined by the taxpayer's:

1. Net profits from self-employment; or
2. Gross income and filing status.

All U.S. citizens and resident immigrants are subject to the filing requirements. Non-citizens who are resident aliens pay US tax on their worldwide income. These restrictions may apply to nonresident aliens (non-U.S. citizens who only pay tax on income earned in the United States) married to U.S. citizens.

Self-Employment Income Threshold
In general, individuals who have net earnings from self-employment of $400 or more must file a tax return and pay self-employment taxes.

Self-employment tax is calculated based on net earnings from self-employment, which is generally equal to 92.35% of the self-employment profits. The self-employment tax rate for 2023 is 15.3%, which includes both the Social Security tax (12.4%) and the Medicare tax (2.9%).

It's important to note that self-employed individuals may be able to deduct certain business expenses, such as home office expenses, supplies, and travel expenses, from their self-employment income. These deductions can help to reduce the amount of self-employment tax that is owed.

> Antoine's only source of income is $1,000 of gross income from self-employment. His business deductions total $580. Self-employment profits are $420 ($1,000 − $580), and net earnings from self-employment are $388 ($420 × 92.35%). Since this amount does not exceed $400, Antoine is not required to file a tax return.

Gross Income Threshold

For tax year 2022, a person who is claimed as a dependent on another taxpayer's return must file a tax return if their gross income exceeds the standard deduction amount for their filing status. The standard deduction amounts for 2022 are:

Single:	*$12,950*
Married filing jointly:	*$25,900*
Married filing separately:	*$12,950*
Head of household:	*$19,400*
Qualifying widow(er) with dependent child:	*$25,900*

If a dependent's gross income is below the standard deduction amount for their filing status, they generally don't need to file a tax return. However, there are some exceptions. For example, a dependent must file a tax return if they have more than $1,100 in unearned income (such as interest and dividends), or if they owe any taxes due to unreported Social Security or Medicare tax on tips or wages.

Additionally, a married dependent who files a separate tax return and wants to claim an itemized deduction must file a tax return if their gross income is $5 or more.

Higher thresholds generally apply to persons who are not claimed as dependents on another's return. Married persons filing separately must file a return when gross income exceeds the exemption amount ($4,050 for 2022). All other persons must file a return when their gross income exceeds the sum of the amounts for taxpayer's personal exemption, basic standard deduction, and additional standard deduction for age. On a joint tax return, the deductions for both spouses count. Neither the additional standard deduction for blindness nor any exemption deductions for dependents are taken into account. Thus, for a married couple filing jointly, where one spouse is 65 and the other is blind, the filing requirement for 2022 is $27,800. This represents a combination of the personal exemption amount, $8,400 (2 × $4,200); the basic standard deduction, $25,900; and the $1,350 additional standard deduction for age.

Who Must File a Tax Return—Rules for Non-dependents.

Gross income thresholds for 2023:

Single	$12,950 ($12,950 + $0)
65 or over	14,600 ($12,950 + $1,650)
Married filing jointly	25,900 ($25,900 + $0)
One 65 or over	27,550 ($25,900 + $1,650)
Both 65 or over	29,200 ($25,900 + $3,300)
Married filing separately	5,000 ($5,000 + $0)

Head of household **65 or over**	19,950 ($19,950 + $0) 21,600 ($19,950 + $1,650)
Qualifying widow(er) **65 or over .**	25,900 ($25,900 + $0) 27,550 ($25,900 + $1,650)

> Note that in determining whether a dependent must file a tax return, the additional standard deduction for both age and blindness increases the gross income threshold. For example, the threshold for a blind, 65-year-old, single person claimed as a dependent on another's return is $4,550 in 2023 if the dependent has no earned income ($1,100 basic standard deduction + $1,700 for age + $1,750 for blindness). Because the personal exemption for a dependent has been suspended, it does not affect a dependent's gross income threshold

Tax Year

Although most people file their taxes using the calendar year, a handful utilize the fiscal year. A fiscal year is used by some businesses and partnerships. Any 12-month term that concludes on the final day of a calendar month other than December is considered a fiscal year. This book assumes that all taxpayers use the calendar year unless otherwise indicated.

Individual tax returns are due on or before the 15th of the fourth month after the end of the fiscal year. This would be April 15 of the next year for calendar year taxpayers. If this date falls on a Saturday, Sunday, or a legal holiday, the deadline is the next working day. A timely return is one that is postmarked on or before the due date, is properly addressed, and includes the correct amount of postage.

Tax Payer Responsibilities

Taxpayers must maintain accurate records to substantiate all things stated on their tax returns. Taxpayers should create and keep an orderly tax record system. This system should make it simple to determine the nature, purpose, and quantity of previous transactions. Invoices, canceled checks, payment receipts, property titles, and copies of past tax returns should be kept in the underlying files.

A well-organized indexing system aids taxpayers in locating archived papers. A robust record-keeping system helps taxpayers avoid forgetting deductions throughout tax season. These documents and receipts must be preserved until the tax return is due. The customary closure date (the final opportunity for the IRS to begin an audit) is three years following the later of I the return's due date (including extensions) or (ii) the date the return was submitted.

For example, if a taxpayer submits a return for the 20x0 tax year before the due date of April 15, 20x1, the 20x0 tax year ends on April 15, 20x4.

The closing date for a tax return that contains an omission of more than 25% of the gross revenue stated on the return is six years after the later of I the due date of the return (including extensions) or (ii) the actual filing date. Thus, if a taxpayer files a return for the year 20x0 before the due date of April 15, 20x1, and the unintentional omission rule for gross income applies, the taxpayer's 20x0 tax year ends on April 15, 20x7.

There is no legislative limit on the amount of extra taxes that can be assessed on a false return. Taxpayers should preserve records of the cost of property (such as stocks and residences) for a longer period of time. Taxpayers are required to record gain (and occasionally loss) on the sale of property. As a result, all property records shall be retained for the longer of I the most recent open tax year or (ii) the year of property disposal plus seven years. A photocopy of the tax return as well as the tax computations should be kept.

Lowering the tax bite

All taxpayers have the right to use all **legal means** to avoid or postpone paying taxes. Taxpayers may be able to lower their tax burden via smart tax preparation. Taxpayers should strive to lower current and future taxes as a primary priority. If feasible, it is often a good idea to postpone taxes to future years.

Get a Good Understanding of The Tax Laws.
The tax laws contain a bewildering amount of regulations that apply to a wide range of personal, company, and financial circumstances. The typical taxpayer should not expect to become even somewhat acquainted with all facets of these laws.

However, the "game of life" includes taxes, and it is impossible to play without a basic understanding of the rules. Taxpayers should concentrate on the laws that affect their own personal and economic situations. Having a basic grasp of these rules is quite advantageous in terms of lowering current and future taxes. It will boost your ability to recognize tax problems. It will also result in better record keeping and less time spent on tax return preparation. Knowledge of tax legislation will offer some comfort to taxpayers who utilize computer tax software that the software generates accurate results.

Although individuals may engage tax consultants to draft their returns, understanding the tax rules should assist people minimize the adviser's fee. Most advisors base their fees on the difficulty and time required to prepare a return. The counsel will not have to charge a fee to explain basic tax regulations to an educated taxpayer.

Chapter 4

Procedures for Tax Determination, Payment, and Reporting

The Internal Revenue Code (Code) specifies the tax rates that taxpayers must use to taxable income in order to calculate their tax due. The present income tax rate system is progressive, meaning that the higher the income, the higher the tax rate. Individual taxpayers are now taxed at the following rates: 10%, 15%, 25%, 28%, 33%, 35%, and 39.6%. These rates are presented by the Internal Revenue Service (IRS) in Tax Rate Schedules and a Tax Table.

Taxpayers must first know their taxable income and filing status in order to calculate their tax. Taxpayers having taxable income of $100,000 or more must utilize the Tax Rate Schedules. Those with taxable income of less than $100,000 must utilize the Tax Table. All Form 1040EZ and Form 1040A filers must use the Tax Table to calculate their tax.

The Tax Rate Schedules

There are four different tax rate schedules, one for each filing status (married filing jointly and qualified widow(er) utilize the same tax rates). The tax rate schedules are more difficult to understand than the Tax Table.

Taxpayers who use a tax rate schedule must compute their tax. The Tax Table does not necessitate any tax computations.

The example below demonstrates how to use the tax rate schedules. Those that use the tax rate schedule to calculate their tax do the following steps:
1. Choose the appropriate rate schedule (based on filing status).
2. Determine the appropriate income range and record both the dollar amount and the tax rate that applies to taxable income in that range.
3. Subtract from taxable income the lowest amount in that income range.
4. Divide the difference from Step 3 by the tax rate from Step 2.
5. Add the amount from Step 4 to the amount from Step 2 to calculate the tax on taxable income.

Using Schedule 1 below, the tax calculation for married couples that file jointly is shown below.

Taxable income (TI)	$100,000		
Less	− 89,450	*	$10,294.00
TI taxed at 25% rate	$ 10,550		
Multiply by rate	× 22%		2,321.00
Tax on TI of $100,000 is			$12,615

Schedule 1

Federal Personal Income Tax Rates for 2023

	Taxable Income		Tax Bracket
	Over	But Not Over	
Single Individuals	$0	$11,000	10% of the taxable income
	$11,000	$44,725	$1,100.00 plus 12% of the excess over $11,000
	$44,725	$95,375	$5,147.50 plus 22% of the excess over $44,725
	$95,375	$182,100	$16,290.00 plus 24% of the excess over $95,375
	$182,100	$231,250	$37,104.00 plus 32% of the excess over $182,100
	$231,250	$578,125	$52,832.00 plus 35% of the excess over $231,250
	$578,125	Over	$174,238.25 plus 37% of the excess over $578,125
	Standard Deduction $13,850		
Married Filing Jointly & Surviving Spouses	$0	$22,000	10% of the taxable income
	$22,000	$89,450	$2,200.00 plus 12% of the excess over $22,000
	$89,450	$190,750	$10,294.00 plus 22% of the excess over $89,450
	$190,750	$364,200	$32,580.00 plus 24% of the excess over $190,750
	$364,200	$462,500	$74,208.00 plus 32% of the excess over $364,200
	$462,500	$693,750	$105,664.00 plus 35% of the excess over $462,500
	$693,750	Over	$186,601.50 plus 37% of the excess over $693,750
	Standard Deduction $27,700		
Married Filing Separately	$0	$11,000	10% of the taxable income
	$11,000	$44,725	$1,100.00 plus 12% of the excess over $11,000
	$44,725	$95,375	$5,147.50 plus 22% of the excess over $44,725
	$95,375	$182,100	$16,290.00 plus 24% of the excess over $95,375
	$182,100	$231,250	$37,104.00 plus 32% of the excess over $182,100
	$231,250	$346,875	$52,832.00 plus 35% of the excess over $231,250
	$346,875	Over	$93,300.75 plus 37% of the excess over $346,875
	Standard Deduction $13,850		
Head of Household	$0	$15,700	10% of the taxable income
	$15,700	$59,850	$1,570.00 plus 12% of the excess over $15,700
	$59,850	$95,350	$6,868.00 plus 22% of the excess over $59,850
	$95,350	$182,100	$14,678.00 plus 24% of the excess over $95,350
	$182,100	$231,250	$35,498.00 plus 32% of the excess over $182,100
	$231,250	$578,100	$51,226.00 plus 35% of the excess over $231,250
	$578,100	Over	$172,623.50 plus 37% of the excess over $578,100
	Standard Deduction $20,800		

Tax Table

Taxpayers with less than $100,000 in taxable income must utilize the Tax Table to calculate their tax. The Tax Table is more user-friendly than the tax rate schedules. Using their taxable income and filing status, taxpayers just locate their tax from the table.

Each filing status has its own column in the Tax Table. A qualified widow(er) fills out the same field as a married couple filing jointly.

The IRS utilizes the tax rate schedules to compute the tax on the midpoint of each income range to establish the Tax Table amounts. The Tax Table indicates a tax of $3,000 for a single person with taxable income of $23,000. This is the tax on $23,025 - the midway between $23,000 and $23,050. This amount is shown in the table on the line that covers taxable income of at least $23,000 but less than $23,050. Because the taxpayer is single, the appropriate tax shows at the intersection of the income range row and the "Single" column.

Paying the Tax Liability

When it comes to paying their tax due, most taxpayers use the tax withholding system imposed on them by their employers. They may also pay estimated taxes. Tax credits, past year overpayments, extra payroll taxes deducted, and payments submitted with individuals' requests to extend the filing date of their tax returns are all variables that might lower tax liabilities. Taxpayers deduct these things from their tax liability to calculate the net amount owed to or from the government.

Federal Taxes Withheld

Employers are required by law to withhold income, social security, and Medicare taxes from wages paid to their employees. The IRS produces tax withholding tables to assist employers in determining the exact amount of federal income tax to withhold. These tables are used by employers in connection with personal information submitted by their workers on Form W-4, Employee's Withholding Allowance Certificate.

Employers calculate the appropriate amount of federal income tax to withhold by cross-referencing the information on the two forms. Employers notify employees of their previous year's earnings and tax withholdings before February 1 of each year. This information is communicated to employees via Form W-2, Wage and Tax Statement. Employees enter their federal income tax withholdings in the "Payments" portion of their tax returns when preparing their federal income tax forms.

Tax Credits

Some tax credits are of a more personal nature. Others are concerned with company operations. Many personal tax credits can be claimed on Form 1040A, but a few can only be reported on Form 1040. The earned income credit is the sole personal tax credit authorized on Form 1040EZ.

Foreign Tax Credits

Individuals and companies are both eligible for the foreign tax credit. Citizens, residents, and domestic corporations in the United States are taxed on their international income. As a result, overseas income may be taxed twice: once by the foreign country and again by the US government. The foreign tax credit decreases the US income tax by the amount of foreign taxes paid. As a result, foreign income is not taxed twice. The foreign tax credit cannot exceed the amount of US taxes paid on overseas income recorded in taxable income. The amount of foreign tax credit is calculated using Form 1116, Foreign Tax Credit. Individuals can also deduct foreign taxes paid as an itemized deduction.

Child and Dependant Care Credit

Individual taxpayers who pay someone to care for a qualified person while they work are eligible for a nonrefundable child and dependent care credit. The credit is calculated as a percentage of qualified costs incurred for the care of one or more qualifying individuals. Depending on the taxpayer's AGI, the percentage utilized to compute the credit ranges from 20% to 35%. Taxpayers with an AGI of less than $15,000 calculate their credit by multiplying their qualifying expenses by 35%. This proportion decreases by 1% for every $2,000 of AGI beyond $15,000, until it hits 20% for taxpayers with AGI in excess of $43,000. Figure 4-1 shows the percentages that apply for each level of AGI.

IF your adjusted gross income is:		THEN the percentage is:
Over	But not over	
$0	$15,000	35%
15,000	17,000	34%
17,000	19,000	33%
19,000	21,000	32%
21,000	23,000	31%
23,000	25,000	30%
25,000	27,000	29%
27,000	29,000	28%
29,000	31,000	27%
31,000	33,000	26%
33,000	35,000	25%
35,000	37,000	24%
37,000	39,000	23%
39,000	41,000	22%
41,000	43,000	21%
43,000	No limit	20%

Figure 4-1; Child and dependant care credit table

Qualifying Person

At least one qualified individual must reside with the taxpayer for more than half of the year in order to claim the child and dependent care credit. A eligible person is defined as follows for the purposes of this credit:

1. A "qualifying child" (as defined in section 108), who is under the age of 13, whom the taxpayer can claim as a dependent,

2. A dependant (of any age) who is physically or mentally unable to give self-care, or

3. A spouse who is physically or mentally unable to provide self-care.

Only the custodial parent can claim the kid as a qualified individual if the parents are divorced or separated.

Even if the custodial parent enables the noncustodial parent to claim the dependency exemption, the kid cannot be claimed as a qualified person by the noncustodial parent (since the child will not have lived with the parent for more than half of the year). When both parents share custody of a kid, the parent who has custody for the majority of the year can claim the child as a qualified person.

Qualified Expenses

Qualified costs for the child and dependent care credit are sums paid by taxpayers for child and dependent care so that they can work, seek for job, or attend education. Payments for domestic services such as cooking and housekeeping can be included as long as the primary purpose for the expenditure was to provide care for an eligible individual.

Qualified costs might be for in-home or out-of-home care supplied by the taxpayer. Payments to relatives are deductible unless the taxpayer lists the relative as a dependant. Payments to the taxpayer's kid who will not be 19 by the end of the year, on the other hand, never qualify as eligible expenses. Payments to the taxpayer's spouse are also not qualifying expenses.

> While Matthew works, he pays his 23-year-old daughter, Mirabel, to watch his 4-year-old son, Tyler. Matthew claims Tyler, but not Mirabel, as a dependent. Payments to Mirabel for Tyler's care are qualified expenses. Had Mirabel not reached the age of 19 by December 31, or had Matthew been able to claim her as a dependent, the payments would not count as qualified expenses.

Qualified expenses must be reduced by nontaxable reimbursements the taxpayer receives from an employer's dependent care assistance plan.

> During the year, Al and Lisa Sherman paid a childcare provider $6,000 to look after their sons (ages 4 and 6) while they worked. Al received a $2,500 nontaxable reimbursement from his employer's dependent care assistance plan. The Shermans' qualified expenses are $3,500 ($6,000 − $2,500).

Limitations on Qualified Expenses

The Code initially caps eligible costs at $3,000 for one qualifying individual ($6,000 for two or more qualifying people). Nontaxable reimbursements from an employer's dependent care assistance plan are deducted from these cash amounts. The Code restricts these sums even further to the taxpayer's earned income.

If the taxpayer is married, the maximum eligible costs are limited to the spouse who has the lower earned income. Thus, the lesser of (i) the taxpayer's qualifying costs less nontaxable reimbursements from a dependent care assistance plan, (ii) the monetary limitations ($3,000/$6,000) minus nontaxable reimbursements, or (iii) the taxpayer's earned income is the maximum qualified expenses.

> Tom paid $2,100 in qualified expenses for the care of his 7-year-old son. Tom's earned income equals $15,500. His maximum qualified expenses are $2,100 [the lesser of (i) qualified expenses of $2,100, (ii) $3,000 limit for one qualifying person, or (iii) earned income of $15,500].

> Same facts as in Example 4, except that during the year Tom received a $1,700 nontaxable reimbursement from his employer's dependent care assistance plan. Tom's maximum qualified expenses are $400 [the lesser of (i) $400 of qualified expenses ($2,100 − $1,700), (ii) $1,300 limit for one qualifying person ($3,000 − $1,700), or (iii) earned income of $15,500].

To claim the child and dependent care credit, a married couple must submit a joint return. In most cases, a taxpayer's spouse must be gainfully employed in order for the pair to qualify for the child and dependent care credit. A unique provision, however, applies to spouses who are either incapacitated or full-time students. For the purposes of the earned income limitation, this rule implies the spouse has some earned income. When the taxpayer has one qualified person, the amount "deemed" earned is $250 per month; when the taxpayer has two or more qualifying people, the amount "deemed" earned is $500 per month.

The sum is "deemed" earned solely during the months when the spouse is a full-time student or unable to care for themselves.

Paul and kate have two children, ages 3 and 5. During the year, Paul worked full-time. Kate did not work, but she attended college full-time 10 months out of the year. They paid $6,600 in qualified childcare expenses. Since their childcare expenses exceed the $6,000 limit for two or more qualifying persons, the qualified expenses are initially limited to $6,000. Even though Kate does not work, she is "deemed" to be employed for 10 months of the year with earnings of $5,000 ($500 × 10 months). Since Kate's "deemed" earnings of $5,000 are less than $6,000, their maximum qualified expenses for purposes of computing the child and dependent care credit are $5,000.

Giving a full-time student spouse who does not work "deemed" earned income allows the couple to claim the child and dependent care credit. Without this special rule, the lesser of qualified expenses, the dollar limits, and earned income would be $0 in situations where the full-time student spouse did not work. However, these "deemed" earnings are not taxable income and are not included in the calculation of the couples' taxable income.

To compute the child and dependent care credit, taxpayers multiply their maximum qualified expenses by the applicable percentage (from Figure 4-1).

Assume that Paul and Kate only source of gross income is Paul's wages of $29,500. Taxpayers with AGI between $29,001 and $31,000 multiply their maximum qualified expenses by 27% (Figure 4-1). Thus, the their nonrefundable child and dependent care credit would equal $1,350 ($5,000 × 27%). Although Kate's "deemed" wages of $5,000 were used in determining the couple's maximum qualified expenses, they are not real wages. Accordingly, they are not used in computing the couple's $29,500 of AGI.

Claiming the Credit

This credit is claimed on Form 2441, Child and Dependent Care Expenses, by taxpayers who submit Form 1040 or Form 1040A. Figure 4-2 depicts the form 2441. The credit for child and dependent care is nonrefundable. The credit amount is restricted to the taxpayer's total tax liability excluding any overseas tax credit claimed. Unused sums cannot be carried forward to next tax year.

Form **2441** — Child and Dependent Care Expenses. Department of the Treasury, Internal Revenue Service (99). 2021. OMB No. 1545-0074. Attachment Sequence No. 21. Attach to Form 1040, 1040-SR, or 1040-NR. Go to www.irs.gov/Form2441 for instructions and the latest information.

Higher Education Credits

Education credits are available to those who pay qualified education costs on behalf of themselves or eligible students during the fiscal year. Education credits are classified into two sorts. The American opportunity credit is one, while the lifelong learning credit is another. Taxpayers cannot claim both credits for the same student in the same year. They can, however, claim both credits in the same year for separate pupils. Once a taxpayer's AGI surpasses a particular threshold, certain credits are no longer accessible. Married couples filing separately are not permitted to claim education credits.

Tuition must generally be paid in the same year that the semester or quarter begins in order to qualify for the credit. Tuition paid in one year for a course that begins within three months of the next year, on the other hand, qualifies for the credit in the year it is paid. Tuition paid in 2021 for classes beginning before April 1, 2022, therefore, counts for the 2021 education credit.

To determine any education credit, only "adjusted qualifying education costs" are utilized. These are the amounts spent out of pocket by the taxpayer for tuition, fees, and course-related materials, supplies, and equipment. As a result, any expenditures incurred as a result of nontaxable scholarships and other tax-free educational advantages cannot be utilized to calculate the credit. This includes funds from an employer's educational aid program.

American Opportunity Credit
The American Opportunity Credit gives a maximum tax credit of $2,500 for each qualifying student. Students are eligible for this credit if they have completed up to five years of post-secondary education. They must also be enrolled in at least half of full-time credit hours during one semester or quarter during the year.

Post-secondary education is the stage of education that follows high school. When students attend universities, academies, colleges, seminaries, technical institutes, vocational or trade schools, and other institutions that give academic degrees or professional certificates, they acquire a postsecondary education.

To compute the amount of the credit, taxpayers add 100% of the first $2,000 of adjusted qualified education expenses to 25% of the lesser of (i) $2,000 or (ii) those expenses in excess of $2,000. The maximum credit is $2,500 [(100% × $2,000) + (25% × $2,000)].

On December 22, 2021, Dwayne paid $800 for his son's tuition for the Spring 2022 semester. The son attends college full-time and is a freshman during the Spring semester. On August 15, 2022, Dwayne paid $840 for his son's Fall 2022 tuition. His American opportunity credit for 2022 equals $840. The $800 paid in 2021 for classes that began before April 1, 2022 qualified for the American opportunity credit in 2021.

For tax year 2021, the income thresholds for reducing the American opportunity credit are as follows:

Single, head of household, or qualifying widow(er): *the credit is gradually reduced if AGI is between $80,000 and $90,000, and is completely phased out if AGI exceeds $90,000.*

Married filing jointly: *the credit is gradually reduced if AGI is between $160,000 and $180,000, and is completely phased out if AGI exceeds $180,000.*

(Married taxpayers who file separately (MFS) cannot take the education credit.)

> Betty reports AGI of $82,330 on her 2020 tax return. In 2020, Betty paid $3,000 in tuition and fees for her dependent son, who is a full-time student attending his fourth year of college. Betty's initial American opportunity credit is $2,250 [($2,000 × 100%) + ($1,000 × 25%)]. However, because AGI exceeds the $80,000 threshold for unmarried taxpayers, Betty must reduce her credit by $524 [$2,250 × ($82,330 − $80,000)/$10,000)]. Betty's American opportunity credit is $1,726 ($2,250 − $524).

40% of the American Opportunity Credit is refundable for the majority of taxpayers. The remaining 60% is a nonrefundable credit that may only be used to a taxpayer's overall income tax burden. In Example above, Betty would record a refundable credit of $690 ($1,726 × 40%) and a nonrefundable credit of $1,036 ($1,726 − $690).

Lifetime Learning Credit
The lifelong learning credit allows for a $2,000 tax credit every year. This is in contrast to the American Opportunity Credit, which has a maximum credit of $2,500 for each qualified student. Other distinctions between the two credits include the following.

1. A student can obtain the lifetime learning credit even if they only attend half-time.
2. Tuition and course-related expenses paid for education beyond the first four years of college are eligible for the lifelong learning credit.
3. The lifetime learning credit is not refundable in any way.

4. *For higher-income taxpayers, lower AGI levels apply to diminish the lifetime learning credit.*

To calculate the lifetime learning credit, taxpayers multiply 20% by the smaller of (i) $10,000 or (ii) the year's adjusted eligible education costs.

> On August 15 2020, Becky paid $3,000 to cover her tuition for the Fall semester. Becky is a graduate student in the nursing program at Arizona State University. Becky's lifetime learning credit for 2020 equals $600 ($3,000 × 20%).

> On December 16, 2020, the Edwards paid $6,000 for their daughter's and $7,000 for their son's Spring 2020 tuition. The Spring semester began on January 21, 2020. Both children attend college less than halftime. The Edwards' lifetime learning credit for 2020 equals $2,000 [(lesser of $10,000 or $13,000) × 20%]. The maximum lifetime learning credit is $2,000 per taxpayer each year.

Taxpayers who are eligible for the lifetime learning credit can claim a maximum of $2,000 per year, per tax return. However, the credit amount may be reduced if the taxpayer's AGI exceeds certain thresholds. For the tax year 2022, single taxpayers with an AGI over $69,000 and married couples filing jointly with an AGI over $138,000 may be subject to a reduction in the credit amount.

Additionally, taxpayers who file as married filing separately are not eligible for the lifetime learning credit.

The phase-out range for the lifetime learning credit has been updated for 2023. For taxpayers whose filing status is single, head of household or qualifying widow(er), the phase-out range is $10,000. Thus, when these taxpayers' AGI exceeds $59,000 ($49,000 + $10,000), their lifetime learning credit is reduced. For married couples filing a joint return, the phase-out range is $20,000. Thus, when their AGI exceeds $118,000 ($98,000 + $20,000), their lifetime learning credit is fully phased-out.

Claiming the Credit

The education credit is claimed on Form 8863, Education Credits (American Opportunity and Lifetime Learning Credits). They begin by filling out Part III of the form (included on page 2) for each student for whom the taxpayer is seeking an education credit.

Part III requires taxpayers to provide the student's name (line 20) and social security number (line 21). They also offer information on the educational institution the student attended as well as if the student got a scholarship that the college reported to the IRS on Form 1098-T. (line 22). They next respond to questions (lines 23–26) that determine whether the taxpayer is eligible to claim the American Opportunity Credit or the Lifetime Learning Credit for the student.

If the student specified in Part III qualifies for the American opportunity credit, the taxpayer enters the adjusted qualifying education costs on line 27, and the initial credit (before any decrease due to excess AGI) is determined by following the instructions on lines 28-30. If the student is eligible for the lifetime learning credit, the modified qualifying education costs are reported on line 31.

After completing page 2 of Form 8863 for each student, the taxpayer totals all eligible costs for each credit and enters the total for the American opportunity credit on Part I. (line 1). The lifetime learning credit total is then recorded on Part II (line 10). The initial lifetime learning credit is restricted to the smaller of the total eligible costs or $10,000 on line 11. Line 12 is filled with 20% of the amount from line 11. This amount is the taxpayer's first lifetime learning credit.

If the taxpayer is claiming the American opportunity credit, follow the instructions on lines 2 through 7 to lower the credit amount when AGI exceeds $80,000 ($160,000 if married filing jointly). Any residual credit on line 7 is multiplied by 40%. This is the fraction of the taxpayer's education credit that is refundable. The nonrefundable part (60%) is recorded in Part II (line 9) and applied to the taxpayer's nonrefundable lifetime learning credit.

If the taxpayer is claiming the lifetime learning credit, follow the instructions on lines 13 through 18 to lower the credit amount when AGI reaches $54,000 ($108,000 if married filing jointly). The smaller of (i) the taxpayer's tax obligation less the foreign tax credit, child and dependent care credit, and elderly or disabled credit, or (ii) the taxpayer's total nonrefundable education credits is the taxpayer's nonrefundable education credit. This determination is made using a Credit Limit Worksheet provided in the Form 8863 instructions. Finally, any refundable credit (from line 8) and nonrefundable credit (from line 19) must be transferred to their corresponding lines on the taxpayer's tax return (Form 1040A or Form 1040).

In 2020, Ed and Sue Reese pay $3,500 for their daughter, Mary's, tuition at Flathead Community College, in Kalispell, MT. Mary is a freshman attending college full-time. Mary did not receive any scholarship income, and the Reeses' 2020 AGI is $174,660. The Reeses' initial American opportunity credit is $2,375 [($2,000 × 100%) + (1,500 × 25%)]. Because their AGI exceeds $160,000, they must reduce their credit by $1,741 ($2,375 × ($14,660 excess AGI/$20,000). The Reeses' education credit for 2020 is $634 ($2,375 – $1,741), of which 40%, or $254, is refundable and the rest ($380) is nonrefundable.

Retirement Savings Contribution Credits

Certain taxpayers may claim a non-refundable tax credit for contributions to retirement savings programs (including amounts deducted from their wages). The credit is in addition to any deduction or exclusion for contributions to a retirement plan. Contributions to regular and Roth IRAs, as well as other qualifying retirement plans such as 401(k) plans, 403(b) annuities, 457 plans, SIMPLE and SEP plans, are eligible for the credit.

Filing Status	AGI Over	AGI Not over	Credit Percentage
Married filing jointly	$0	$40,000	50%
	$40,000	$43,000	20%
	$43,000	$66,000	10%
	Above $66,000		0%
Head of Household	$0	$30,000	50%
	$30,000	$32,250	20%
	$32,250	$49,500	10%
	$49,500		0%
All Others	$0	$20,000	50%
	$20,000	$21,500	20%
	$21,500	$33,000	10%
	Above $33,000		0%

Table 4-1:Retirement Savings Contributions Credit (also known as the Saver's Credit) for the tax year 2023.

Note: AGI refers to adjusted gross income. The credit percentage is a percentage of the taxpayer's eligible contribution amount, up to a maximum credit of $1,000 for individuals and $2,000 for married couples filing jointly.

To be eligible for the credit, taxpayers must be at least 18 years old. Furthermore, no credit is provided for individuals listed as dependents or full-time students. As shown in Figure 4-1, no credit is available for joint filers with AGI in excess of

$66,000; head of household filers with AGI in excess of $49,500; or all other filers with AGI in excess of $33,000 (this includes taxpayers filing as single, married filing separately, or qualifying widow(er)).

Claiming the Credit
The credit for qualified retirement savings contributions is calculated using Form 8880, Credit for Qualified Retirement Savings Contributions.

The credit is subsequently recorded on Form 1040A or Form 1040 with the taxpayer's other nonrefundable tax credits on Form 1040A or Form 1040. The credit amount is restricted to the taxpayer's total tax due after deducting the nonrefundable tax credits listed below: foreign tax credit, child and dependent care credit, and education credit.

> Chris and Megan Evans report $37,200 of AGI on their 2021 joint return. During the year Chris contributed $5,000 to his Roth IRA. The Evans' retirement savings contributions credit equals $1000 ($2,000 per taxpayer maximum × 50% from table4-1 . Assuming the Evans do not have any other nonrefundable tax credits for the year, they report this amount on Form 1040 or Form 1040A.

> Same facts as above, except that in addition to the retirement savings contributions credit, the Evans claim a $1,000 education credit. The Evans' total tax liability for 2020 is $1,298. Once the Orrs reduce their tax liability by the $1,000 education credit, only $298 of tax liability remains. Their retirement savings contributions credit will be limited to $298. Since the retirement savings contributions credit is nonrefundable, the Orrs receive no tax benefit from the $702 ($1000 − $298) unused portion of the credit.

Child Tax Credit (CTC)

For tax year 2021, the Child Tax Credit has been increased to a maximum of $3,000 per qualifying child between the ages of 6 and 17, and $3,600 for children under 6. Additionally, the age limit for qualifying children has been increased to 18 and full-time students between the ages of 19 and 24. The credit is fully refundable for those who are eligible.

There have also been changes to the income limits for the Child Tax Credit. For tax year 2021, the credit begins to phase out for single filers with an AGI of $75,000, head-of-household filers with an AGI of $112,500, and married filing jointly filers with an AGI of $150,000. The credit is completely phased out for single filers with an AGI of $200,000, head-of-household filers with an AGI of $200,000, and married filing jointly filers with an AGI of $400,000. The taxpayer loses $50 of the credit for each $1,000 (or portion thereof) that AGI exceeds the threshold amount.

> Tom and Carol Normand file a joint tax return. They claim their two children, ages 8 and 9, as dependents. Because the Normands' AGI of $116,400 is within the $150,000 threshold for MFJ, they are entitled to the full $3,000 CTC.

Note: The phase out of the CTC is $50 per $1,000 of excess AGI (or portion thereof). How quickly the taxpayer's CTC is phased out depends on the amount of AGI, the taxpayer's filing status, and the number of qualifying children.

John files as head of household and claims his 10-year-old nephew as a dependent. John's AGI is $120,530. Since a nephew is a qualifying child, Since John files as head of household and claims his 10-year-old nephew as a dependent, he may be eligible for the CTC. Since his nephew is 10 years old, John can claim a maximum credit of $3,000 for him.

The phase-out of the CTC for head of household filers with one qualifying child begins at $112,500 of AGI, and is reduced by $50 for every $1,000 of AGI above that threshold. Since John's AGI is $120,530, his CTC will be reduced by $4,015 (($120,530 - $112,500)÷1,000 x $50).

Therefore, John's CTC for his 10-year-old nephew will be $3,000 - $4,015 = -$1,015, which means he will not be eligible for the credit.

Claiming the Credit

While the CTC is normally nonrefundable, certain taxpayers may be eligible for a refundable credit. However, before calculating the refundable component of the CTC, taxpayers must first calculate the nonrefundable portion of the CTC. This is done on the Child Tax Credit Worksheet, which may be found in the Form 1040 instructions.

This worksheet deducts the following nonrefundable personal credits from the taxpayer's total tax liability: foreign tax credit, child and dependent care credit, nonrefundable education credit, old or disabled credit, and retirement savings contributions credit. The nonrefundable element of the credit is the smaller of (i) the remaining tax due or (ii) the taxpayer's CTC. Nonrefundable CTCs are reported on Form 1040A or Form 1040 together with other nonrefundable tax credits.

The Scotts file a joint return. They claim their three children (all under age 17) as dependents. The Stewarts' AGI is $80,970 and their total tax liability is $8,166. They are only entitled to one tax credit—the CTC. Since the Scotts' AGI is less than $150,000, they do not lose any of their $9,000 CTC ($3,000 × 3 qualifying children) due to excess AGI. The Scotts report the entire $3,000 CTC as a nonrefundable credit.

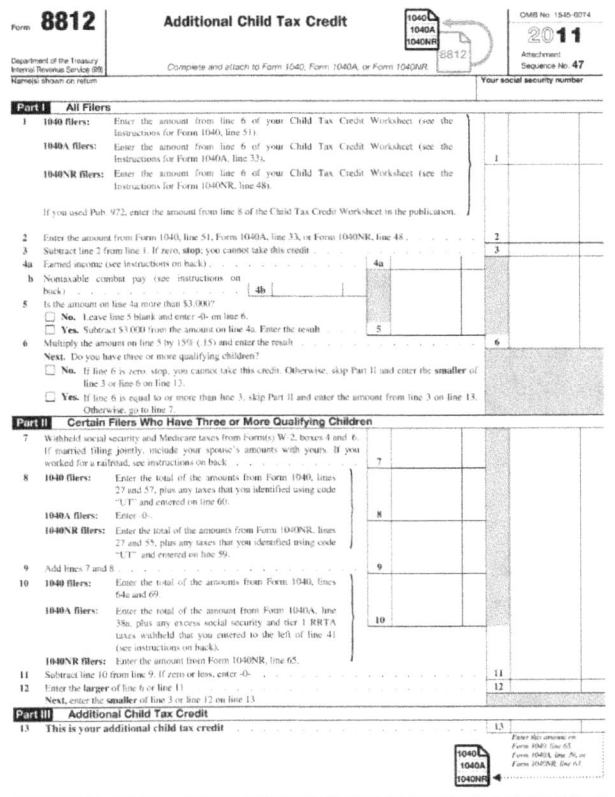

Residential Energy Credit

The residential energy efficient property credit provides taxpayers with a tax credit for installing alternative energy equipment in any home that they own in the United States. As a result, the credit can be used for installations made to the taxpayer's primary residence as well as any vacation house owned by the taxpayer.

Solar hot water heaters, solar electric equipment, and wind turbines are examples of qualified property. The credit is equal to 26% of the cost of the alternative energy equipment. This credit has no monetary limit. Furthermore, if the amount of the credit exceeds the taxpayer's outstanding tax burden, the excess can be carried over to the following tax year, which is a unique characteristic of this nonrefundable credit. Subtracting all additional nonrefundable credits from the taxpayer's total tax burden yields the remaining tax liability.

Adoption Credit

For eligible adoption expenditures, taxpayers can claim a nonrefundable tax credit. For adoptions of US citizens or residents, the credit is taken only if the adoption is finalized in that year or was finalized in a previous year. Otherwise, the credit is applied to the year after the year in which the costs were paid. This is sometimes referred to as the one-year delay rule. When adoption expenditures are spread over more than one year, the credit is calculated using the restrictions in place in the year the adoption is finalized. The adoption credit can be claimed for adoptions of US citizens or residents even if the adoption is never finalized. Adoption credits for foreign children can only be claimed once the adoption is finalized.

The adoption tax credit is restricted to the first $14,440 of qualifying adoption expenditures in 2021. The credit is also refundable, which means that taxpayers may claim it even if they owe no taxes. For taxpayers with modified AGI of more than $216,660, the credit begins to taper out and is totally phased out for taxpayers with modified AGI of more than $256,660.

Furthermore, the credit is accessible for both domestic and foreign adoptions in 2021, and it may be claimed in the year the adoption is finalized. Taxpayers may be entitled to claim a credit for certain costs incurred in the previous year if the adoption is not yet final. Those with an excess of modified AGI (AGI + any overseas earned income exclusion) lose their credit by the following amount: **(the lesser of $14,440 or qualified expenses) × (excess modified AGI ÷ $40,000)**

Qualified adoption costs are those directly associated to the legal adoption of a child who is either under the age of 18 at the time of the adoption or who is physically or mentally incapable of self-care. Adoption expenses that are reasonable and necessary, court charges, and attorney's fees are examples of such expenditures. Nontaxable reimbursements from an employer's adoption assistance plan must be deducted from both the eligible adoption expenditures and the $14,440 maximum.

In 2020, the Fernandes paid $14,000 in qualified adoption expenses. The adoption was finalized in 2021. Their modified AGI in 2020 was $169,450. It was $215,994 in 2021. Since the adoption was not finalized in 2020, how much adoption credit can they claim in 2021 (under the one-year delay rule).

The first step is to determine the credit limit for 2021, which is $13,400 (the 2021 limit of $14,440 reduced by the inflation adjustment).

Next, the amount of the credit must be reduced because their modified AGI exceeds the phase-out threshold of $211,160 for 2021. The excess modified AGI is $4,834 ($215,994 - $211,160), and the reduction is calculated as follows:
($13,400 × $4,834 ÷ $40,000) = $1,621.32

Therefore, the maximum adoption credit the Fernandes can claim in 2021 is:
$13,400 - $1,621.32 = $11,778.68

So they can claim a credit of $11,778.68 for their adoption expenses in 2021.

Claiming the Credit

Adoption credit claimants must file Form 8839, Qualified Adoption Expenses. They then add their adoption credit, along with any other nonrefundable credits, on Form 1040. They must also provide documentation that their expenditures have been paid. Taxpayers who are unable to use the full amount of their adoption credit (because to the fact that it is a nonrefundable credit) can carry it over for five years.

Earned Income Credit

The earned income credit (EIC) is a refundable tax credit that gives lower-income employees tax relief. By claiming the EIC, taxpayers who report a small amount of earned income may actually receive money back from the government. This occurs when their EIC balance surpasses their tax liability. The EIC was created by Congress to encourage people to enter the labor field. Within restrictions, when a person's earned income (wages) rises, so does the amount of the EIC. The EIC's goal is to encourage individuals to look for work.

Taxpayers Eligible for the Credit
The EIC is not available to married persons using the married filing separately filing status, or to anyone claimed as a dependent on another taxpayer's return. Taxpayers with disqualified income in excess of $10,000 (adjusted annually for inflation) cannot take the EIC. Disqualified income includes dividends, interest (including tax-exempt interest), net rental income, and capital gains.

1. Be between the ages of 25 and 64 at the conclusion of the tax year, not be claimed as a dependant by another person, and have spent more than half of the year in the United States, or
2. Have a "qualifying child."

A qualified kid must be less than the taxpayer's age. When claiming the EIC for an eligible kid, taxpayers must include the child's name, age, and social security number (SSN). If any of these are not presented, the EIC for that kid will be refused. A qualified kid was described in Chapter 1 as someone who meets six criteria: relationship, age, residency, support, joint return, and citizenship. Only the first three of these standards must be met by a "qualified kid" for the purposes of the EIC (relationship, age, and residency).

An unmarried individual does not have to be the taxpayer's dependant to be a qualified child for EIC purposes, but a married person must. When the dependency exemption for a married kid has been granted to the noncustodial parent, the custodial parent may claim a married child as a qualified child (and claim the EIC for that child).

If the parents are divorced or separated and the kid is a qualifying child for both parents, the child is classified as the custodial parent's qualifying child. If there is no custodial parent, the parent with the greatest AGI is entitled to the child's EIC. In other cases, if the kid qualifies for more than one taxpayer, the credit is given to the child's parent.

If neither individual is the child's parent, the taxpayer with the greatest AGI is entitled to the child's EIC. These tie-break standards are the same ones used to determine who can claim the dependency exemption for a qualified kid.

> Jake and his 5-year-old son live with Jake's father, Frank, for the whole year. Jake's AGI is $15,000, and Frank's AGI is $20,000. The son is a qualifying child to both Jake and Frank. Since Jake is the parent, he claims the EIC.

Credit Rates and Dollar Amounts

In general, when taxable earned income rises, so does the EIC. However, when income surpasses a specific threshold, the credit is tapered away. This phase-down is determined by the greater of earned income or AGI. The Earned Income Credit Worksheet is used by taxpayers to calculate the correct EIC using the Earned Income Credit tables. This worksheet is kept by taxpayers for their records. Those with qualifying children, on the other hand, must additionally complete and attach Schedule EIC, Earned Income Credit, to their tax filings.

Earned income comprises all sorts of taxable pay as well as net profits from self-employment for the purposes of the EIC. Nontaxable employee pay does not include salary deferrals under retirement plans, salary reductions under cafeteria programs, or any dependent care, adoption, or educational aid benefits. Retirement income, social security or unemployment payments, or alimony are also not considered earned income. Taxpayers will have at least $1 of earned income credit as long as they have earned income and their earned income or AGI (whichever is greater) does not exceed the following amounts.

	Married Filing Jointly	All Other Taxpayers
No Children	$21,920	$15,980
One Qualifying Children	$47,915	$42,258
Two Qualifying Children	$53,330	$47,642
Three or More Qualifying Children	$56,884	$51,464

SCHEDULE EIC (Form 1040) Department of the Treasury Internal Revenue Service (99)	**Earned Income Credit** Qualifying Child Information ▶ Complete and attach to Form 1040 or 1040-SR only if you have a qualifying child. ▶ Go to www.irs.gov/ScheduleEIC for the latest information.	OMB No. 1545-0074 **2021** Attachment Sequence No. **43**

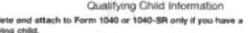 

Name(s) shown on return | | Your social security number

If you are separated from your spouse, filing a separate return and meet the requirements to claim the EIC (see instructions), check here ▶ ☐

Before you begin:
- See the instructions for Form 1040, lines 27a, 27b, and 27c, to make sure that (a) you can take the EIC, and (b) you have a qualifying child.
- Be sure the child's name on line 1 and social security number (SSN) on line 2 agree with the child's social security card. Otherwise, at the time we process your return, we may reduce your EIC. If the name or SSN on the child's social security card is not correct, call the Social Security Administration at 800-772-1213.
- If you have a child who meets the conditions to be your qualifying child for purposes of claiming the EIC, but that child doesn't have an SSN as defined in the instructions for Form 1040, lines 27a, 27b, and 27c, see the instructions.

- You can't claim the EIC for a child who didn't live with you for more than half of the year.
- If your child doesn't have an SSN as defined in the instructions for Form 1040, lines 27a, 27b, and 27c, see the instructions.
- If you take the EIC even though you are not eligible, you may not be allowed to take the credit for up to 10 years. See the instructions for details.
- It will take us longer to process your return and issue your refund if you do not fill in all lines that apply for each qualifying child.

Qualifying Child Information	Child 1		Child 2		Child 3	
1 Child's name If you have more than three qualifying children, you have to list only three to get the maximum credit.	First name	Last name	First name	Last name	First name	Last name
2 Child's SSN The child must have an SSN as defined in the instructions for Form 1040, lines 27a, 27b, and 27c, unless the child was born and died in 2021 or you are claiming the self-only EIC (see instructions). If your child was born and died in 2021 and did not have an SSN, enter "Died" on this line and attach a copy of the child's birth certificate, death certificate, or hospital medical records showing a live birth.						

Chapter 5

Personal Itemized Deduction

Individuals are often not permitted to deduct personal costs on their tax returns under most circumstances. However, there are several exceptions. As itemized deductions, you can deduct a variety of personal costs. If the standard deduction is more than the itemized deduction, taxpayers may choose to take that instead.

Individuals can make two sorts of deductions. The first kind cuts gross revenue to produce adjusted gross income (AGI). This sort of deduction includes expenses made in a trade or business. Deductions for AGI were covered in the previous chapter. The other kind of deduction (including itemized deductions) lowers AGI. Deductions for AGI are the most desirable deductions. One reason for this is that the tax code utilizes AGI as a foundation to limit certain deductions from AGI. Medical costs and personal casualty losses, for example, are only deductible to the extent that they exceed 10% of AGI. As a result, the lower the AGI, the higher the possibilities of claiming these itemized deductions.

Another reason AGI deductions are favoured is because more than 60% of all taxpayers take the standard deduction rather than itemizing deductions. Having costs that are deductible as itemized deductions does not assist taxpayers who use the (higher) standard deduction. As a result, taxpayers should seek for strategies to maximize their AGI deductions.

Chapter 5 discusses the most typical Schedule A personal deductions, such as medical bills, taxes, interest, charitable donations, and casualty or theft losses. The chapter also discusses how higher-income taxpayers' total itemized deductions are reduced.

For individuals who itemize, the tax regulations normally enable taxpayers to deduct only their own expenses paid with their own money. Only in limited instances is it feasible for taxpayers to obtain deductions for costs they pay on behalf of other individuals. These exceptions are discussed in the chapter.

Reporting Itemized Deductions

Taxpayers usually deduct the larger of either the standard deduction or the total amount of itemized deductions. However, recall from earlier chapters that when spouses file separately and one spouse itemizes deductions, the other spouse must also itemize, even if that amount is $0. Taxpayers that itemize show their deductions on Schedule A.

For some deductions, an extra form must be completed to support the amount reported on Schedule A. Examples include Form 4952 (Investment Interest), Form 8283 (Non-cash Charitable Contributions), Form 4684 (Casualty and Theft Losses), and Form 2106 (Employee Business Expenses).

Itemized Deductions Reported on Schedule A
Medical and Dental Expenses Taxes You Paid
Interest You Paid
Gifts to Charity
Casualty and Theft
Losses
Job Expenses and Certain Miscellaneous
Deductions
Other Miscellaneous Deductions

SCHEDULE A (Form 1040)	**Itemized Deductions**	OMB No. 1545-0074
Department of the Treasury Internal Revenue Service (99)	► Go to www.irs.gov/ScheduleA for instructions and the latest information. ► Attach to Form 1040 or 1040-SR. Caution: If you are claiming a net qualified disaster loss on Form 4684, see the instructions for line 16.	2021 Attachment Sequence No. 07
Name(s) shown on Form 1040 or 1040-SR		Your social security number

Medical and Dental Expenses	**Caution:** Do not include expenses reimbursed or paid by others.	
	1 Medical and dental expenses (see instructions)	1
	2 Enter amount from Form 1040 or 1040-SR, line 11 **2**	
	3 Multiply line 2 by 7.5% (0.075)	3
	4 Subtract line 3 from line 1. If line 3 is more than line 1, enter -0-	4
Taxes You Paid	5 State and local taxes.	
	a State and local income taxes or general sales taxes. You may include either income taxes or general sales taxes on line 5a, but not both. If you elect to include general sales taxes instead of income taxes, check this box ►	5a
	b State and local real estate taxes (see instructions)	5b
	c State and local personal property taxes	5c
	d Add lines 5a through 5c	5d
	e Enter the smaller of line 5d or $10,000 ($5,000 if married filing separately)	5e
	6 Other taxes. List type and amount ►	6
	7 Add lines 5e and 6	7
Interest You Paid **Caution:** Your mortgage interest deduction may be limited (see instructions).	8 Home mortgage interest and points. If you didn't use all of your home mortgage loan(s) to buy, build, or improve your home, see instructions and check this box ►	
	a Home mortgage interest and points reported to you on Form 1098. See instructions if limited	8a
	b Home mortgage interest not reported to you on Form 1098. See instructions if limited. If paid to the person from whom you bought the home, see instructions and show that person's name, identifying no., and address ►	8b
	c Points not reported to you on Form 1098. See instructions for special rules	8c
	d Mortgage insurance premiums (see instructions)	8d
	e Add lines 8a through 8d	8e
	9 Investment interest. Attach Form 4952 if required. See instructions.	9
	10 Add lines 8e and 9	10
Gifts to Charity **Caution:** If you made a gift and got a benefit for it, see instructions.	11 Gifts by cash or check. If you made any gift of $250 or more, see instructions	11
	12 Other than by cash or check. If you made any gift of $250 or more, see instructions. You **must** attach Form 8283 if over $500	12
	13 Carryover from prior year	13
	14 Add lines 11 through 13	14
Casualty and Theft Losses	15 Casualty and theft loss(es) from a federally declared disaster (other than net qualified disaster losses). Attach Form 4684 and enter the amount from line 18 of that form. See instructions	15
Other Itemized Deductions	16 Other—from list in instructions. List type and amount ►	16
Total Itemized Deductions	17 Add the amounts in the far right column for lines 4 through 16. Also, enter this amount on Form 1040 or 1040-SR, line 12a	17
	18 If you elect to itemize deductions even though they are less than your standard deduction, check this box ►	

For Paperwork Reduction Act Notice, see the Instructions for Forms 1040 and 1040-SR.   Cat. No. 17145C   Schedule A (Form 1040) 2021

Medical and Dental Expenses

The medical and dental deduction is available to taxpayers who itemize deductions on their tax return, and it allows them to deduct certain unreimbursed medical and dental expenses that exceed a certain threshold. For most taxpayers, this threshold is 10% of their AGI (adjusted gross income). However, for taxpayers who are age 65 and older, the threshold is lowered to 7.5% of their AGI for the years 2013 to 2020. From 2021 and beyond, the 10% threshold applies to all taxpayers, regardless of age.

On a joint tax return, just one spouse must meet the 10% AGI level. Normally, taxpayers cannot deduct costs paid on behalf of others. The Internal Revenue Code (Code) does, however, enable taxpayers to deduct medical and dental costs paid on behalf of dependents. They can also deduct medical and dental expenditures paid for other people who are not dependents, as long as the person either (1) meets the citizenship, relationship, and support standards, or (2) meets the citizenship and relationship tests for a qualified kid.

Thus, a taxpayer can deduct monies paid for her father's prescription medicines, but she cannot claim him as a dependant since his total income exceeds $3,950. Similarly, a taxpayer can deduct medical expenditures paid on behalf of the taxpayer's sister, who cannot be claimed as a dependant since she provides more than half of her own support for the year. (Recall that siblings satisfy the relationship requirement for a qualified kid).

When one spouse incurs significant medical expenses, it may be beneficial for the couple to file separate tax returns. In this case, the AGI floor for deducting medical expenses would apply to the income of the spouse who incurred the expenses, which would result in a lower floor and a larger potential deduction. This is because the lower income reported on a separate return would reduce the AGI, making it more likely that the medical expenses will exceed the AGI floor. However, it's important to consider other tax implications of filing separately, such as the potential loss of certain tax credits and deductions.

Prescription Drugs & Insulin

Prescription medications are the only medical costs that are deductible. Over-the-counter medications, even if prescribed, do not qualify as a deductible medical cost. Iron and calcium supplements, gluten-free meals, birth control devices, cold treatments, aspirin, allergy drugs, and antacid pills are some of the most often used over-the-counter (nondeductible) recommended goods.

For Jackson's cold and fever, a doctor prescribed an antibiotic and an over-the-counter cold remedy. Steven's co-pay for the antibiotic was $25. The insurance company paid the rest. The cold remedy cost $5. Only the $25 paid for the antibiotic may be deducted.

Medical and Dental Insurance Premiums

Medical expenditures include insurance premiums paid for medical and dental treatment, as well as sums paid through workplace payroll deductions. Medicare premiums withdrawn from the taxpayer's monthly social security payments, as well as monies paid by social security beneficiaries to enhance their Medicare coverage, are also deductible. Premiums for long-term care insurance are also deductible.

Self-employed taxpayers deduct AGI insurance premiums paid during months when the taxpayer (and, if married, the taxpayer's spouse) is not qualified for an employer's medical plan. Any premiums paid by self-employed taxpayers that are not deductible for AGI are deducted on Schedule A as a medical expenditure (line 1).

Premiums spent for the medical element of vehicle insurance, life insurance premiums, and premiums paid for insurance that covers lost wages or loss of a limb or sight are not deductible as medical expenses. Taxpayers cannot also deduct insurance payments paid on their behalf by their employers.

> The Watsons' medical and dental insurance premiums for the year total $24,930. Steven paid $9,972 of this amount through payroll deductions. His employer paid the rest. During the year, the They also paid $1,200 for life insurance and $600 for disability insurance. Only the $9,972 of health insurance premiums Steven paid counts as a medical deduction. The $14,958 of premiums paid by the employer is a tax-free fringe benefit

Other Medical Expenses

Direct payments to medical professionals, such as physicians, dentists, nurses, hospitals, and clinics, can be deducted by taxpayers. Payments paid to qualified Christian Science practitioners, chiropractors, osteopaths, and therapists are also deductible. Lab work, medical treatments, X-rays, CAT scans, and MRIs are all examples of deductible medical care.

Some therapies aimed to help individuals quit smoking are also deductible as medical expenses. This involves taking part in a quit-smoking program. It also covers the purchase of medications that require a doctor's prescription to alleviate the symptoms of nicotine withdrawal.

Taxpayers can deduct the expense of a weight-loss program if it is used to treat a specific ailment that has been identified by a doctor (e.g. obesity, hypertension, or heart disease). They cannot deduct the expense of a weight-loss program if the goal is to improve one's looks, general health, or sense of well-being.

Cosmetic surgery is deductible only when it is medically required, such as to cure a congenital defect or to repair damage caused by injury or sickness. Cosmetic surgery performed for personal (vanity) motives is not deductible.

Nursing Home Care
Depending on the condition of the resident and the services provided by the institution, the full sum paid to the facility may be deductible. When the primary reason for the stay is a medical issue, the taxpayer deducts all costs, including the cost of meals and housing. Alzheimer's illness, paralysis, alcoholism, drug rehabilitation, and a physical disability or handicap are among conditions that qualify for 100% medical care. If the primary reason for residing in the house is for personal care

or family convenience, the taxpayer simply deducts the particular medical costs. Amounts paid for eligible long-term care, on the other hand, are deductible when such services are required by a chronically sick individual.

School for the Handicapped
Amounts paid to send a mentally or physically challenged spouse or disabled dependent to a special school or facility are medical expenses that can be deducted. The primary goal of the school must be to assist students in compensating for or overcoming issues in order for them to operate better.

Employee Physicals
Many people who work with hazardous products or in hazardous jobs get annual physicals. When physicals are required by the employer, the charges are deducted as miscellaneous employee business expenditures. Employees who obtain physicals on their own can deduct the price as a medical expense.

Travel and Transportation
To determine deductible expenditures when traveling to obtain medical care, taxpayers may use either the normal mileage rate or actual expenses. However, because the medical expenditure rate is no longer increased annually, the charge for 2022 will be $.16 per mile, the same as in 2021. Tolls and parking fees are still applied to this figure.

Individuals may deduct their actual expenditures, although the standard mileage rate is more convenient to apply. Only out-of-pocket costs may be deducted when using the actual expense approach. Taxpayers are required to keep a diary of their mileage and costs, as well as receipts for any products purchased. Parents may deduct a child's expenditures under the unique provision that allows a taxpayer to deduct the expenses of others. For example, parents can deduct the cost of traveling their child from Los Angeles to San Diego to see a specialist about their child's ailment.

A travel expenditure deduction is provided when a patient and/or the taxpayer needs travel overnight for medical treatments. The Code restricts accommodation to $50 per night per person.

Capital Expenditures
When prescribed by a medical professional as part of a specific therapy, house renovations and special equipment placed in a home may be deducted. Swimming pools, air conditioners, and elevators are three popular upgrades.

No medical deduction is permitted if the improvement enhances the value of the residence by more than the cost of the improvement. The taxpayer will be reimbursed if the house is eventually sold for a higher price. When the expenditure exceeds the rise in house value, the excess is deducted as a medical expense.

> Under a doctor's prescription for a medical condition, the Kenyons pay $7,000 for a hot tub. The hot tub increases the value of the home by $4,000. The Neals' medical expense for the hot tub is $3,000. They add this amount to their other unreimbursed medical expenses on Schedule A (line 1).

There is an exemption for modifications that allow a physically disabled person to live freely. Building ramps, extending hallways and entrances for wheelchair access, installing support bars and railings, and changing outlets and fixtures are some examples. For tax reasons, the IRS considers the expenses of these sorts of modifications to add no value to the residence. As a result, the full cost of the renovation is tax deductible.

> Walden (age 36) is confined to a wheelchair. In order to live alone,he pays $10,000 to have entrance ramps, bars and railings installed in her home. Although these features are estimated to add as much as $2,000 to the value of her home, the IRS treats their added value as $0. This allows Walden to deduct the full $10,000 as a medical expense deduction. He adds this to his other unreimbursed medical expenses. He then reduces the total by 10% of her AGI.

Other Expenditures

Eye tests, eyeglasses, contact lenses, noncosmetic dental procedures (crowns, dentures, braces, etc.), crutches, canes, wheelchairs, and guide dogs are all routinely deductible medical costs. Nondeductible medical expenses include subscriptions to health clubs, massages, burial and funeral charges, and illicit substances or operations.

Reimbursements

The amount of all eligible medical costs minus any reimbursements constitutes a taxpayer's medical and dental expense deduction. Schedule A shows this net amount (line 1).

There are two scenarios in which medical reimbursements become taxable. First, when an employer-provided insurance coverage reimburses more than the actual medical expenditures incurred, the excess is taxed. (The surplus is not taxed when the employee pays the premium.) Second, if the taxpayer claims a medical deduction and receives a reimbursement the following year, all or a portion of that reimbursement may be taxed under the tax advantage rule. This regulation mandates that taxpayers report the reimbursement in gross income only when they benefitted from deducting medical costs in an earlier year

Taxes you Paid

The tax code restricts the sorts of taxes that can be deducted. Income taxes and property taxes are itemized deductions when collected by a government entity other than the federal government.

Before a tax deduction is allowed, qualifying taxes must fulfill two requirements. First and foremost, the taxpayer must pay the taxes. Second, the taxes paid must be the taxpayer's own. Amounts paid for someone else's taxes cannot be deducted by the taxpayer.

Federal income taxes, FICA (social security and Medicare) taxes, federal and state estate, gift, or inheritance taxes, and use and excise taxes (taxes placed on fuel, cigarettes, and alcohol) are all nondeductible. The rest of this section discusses the several types of taxes that can be claimed as an itemized deduction on Schedule A.

State and Local Taxes

State and local income taxes paid can be deducted on Schedule A. State and local income taxes can be paid in three ways. These are as follows: (1) by W-2 (paycheck) withholdings, (2) by making anticipated tax payments in the current tax year, and (3) by paying additional taxes (but not interest or penalties) for prior or current years.

The provision allowing taxpayers to deduct either state and local income taxes or general sales taxes was made permanent with the passage of the Protecting Americans from Tax Hikes (PATH) Act of 2015. This means that taxpayers can continue to choose to deduct the greater of their state and local income taxes or their general sales taxes paid on their federal tax return. However, the state and local tax (SALT) deduction is capped at $10,000 for tax years 2018 through 2025 due to changes made by the Tax Cuts and Jobs Act of 2017

Refund of State and Local Income Taxes

A refund of state or local income taxes paid in the previous year does not lower the amount of taxes paid during the year. Instead, if the refund is due to taxes deducted in a previous tax year, it is recorded on Form 1040 (page 1) as "Taxable refunds, etc." in line with the tax benefit rule.

> During 20x1, Jason's employer withheld $3,600 for state income taxes from his wages. Jason's itemized deductions in 20x1 exceeded his standard deduction by $8,000. In April of 20x2, Jason files his state income tax return. Two months later he receives a $700 refund. Since Jason's tax liability was lowered in 20x1 when he deducted the $3,600 as an itemized deduction, he reports the $700 in gross income in 20x2. The tax benefit rule taxes Jason on the lesser of (i) the $700 refund, or (ii) the $8,000 excess of his 20x1 itemized deductions over his standard deduction amount.

Real Estate Tax

Individuals can deduct ad valorem taxes paid to state and municipal governments from their AGI under the tax regulations. Ad valorem taxes are levied on the basis of the property's worth.

Local governments charge real estate taxes on property owners depending on the property's value. As a result, the owners can deduct state and local property taxes as an itemized deduction. They can also deduct foreign government real estate taxes.

When selling real estate during the year, the seller is responsible for the real estate taxes up to the day of the transaction. The buyer assumes responsibility on the day of the transaction. Ordinarily, real estate taxes are evaluated once a year. The property owner receives the tax bill. Tax regulations allow taxpayers to deduct costs for which they are both accountable and pay.

When real estate is sold during the year, the person responsible for paying the real estate tax bill may not be the same as the party responsible for paying all of the taxes. Only the percentage of the taxes that the owner is accountable for can be deducted in these cases. To avoid losing deductions, sellers must remit to purchasers their share of real estate taxes up to the date of sale when real estate is sold. Most sales contracts contain standard wording to that effect.

Owners of condominiums and cooperative housing can deduct their part of the real estate taxes paid on these buildings. When the homeowners association pays real estate taxes, it must identify the actual pass-through of property taxes in order to give proof for the tax reduction to the owners. Special assessments, which are added to the property tax bill for local improvements such as roadways, sidewalks, and sewers, are not deductible taxes. These sums are instead added to the owner's basis (investment) in the property.

> On May 11, 20x1, Jill sells her home to the Ryans for $200,000. Real estate taxes on the home are expected to be $3,000 for 20x1. At the closing, Jill pays the Ryans $1,068 ($3,000 × 130/365). This amount is her share of the real estate taxes for the 130 days she owned the home during 20x1. In turn, Jill deducts this amount as real estate taxes on Schedule A in 20x1. At the end of the year, the local government sends the Ryans the tax bill for 20x1. Although they will pay the entire amount due, the Ryans' out-of-pocket costs will be the amount paid minus the $1,068 they received from Jill at the closing. This net amount is the Ryans' share of the real estate taxes. They deduct this amount as real estate taxes on Schedule A in 20x1.

> During the year, the Watsons paid real estate taxes on their main home ($6,405), their vacation home ($3,322), and on a vacant lot they own as an investment ($756). They report the $10,483 total real estate taxes paid on Schedule A (line 6). The tax law does not limit the number of properties on which real estate taxes can be deducted.

Personal Property Tax

Real estate is not the sole sort of property subject to a property tax. Personal property taxes are levied in several states. Personal property refers to all non-real estate property for tax purposes. This implies that all property that is not land or a structure is referred to as personal property.

Personal property can be owned by both individuals and businesses. People might possess personal property for personal use or for financial purposes. Clothing, house furnishings, artwork, and stock shares are examples of such items. Trucks, office furniture, and machinery are examples of personal property that businesses may hold.

Personal property is distinct from the property that individuals own and utilize in their own life. This is known as personal-use property. Property can also be used for commercial or investment purposes. Personal property taxes paid by states and municipalities are deductible if the tax base equals the value of the property. Furthermore, the tax must be levied on an annual basis, regardless of how frequently it is collected.

Personal property may be both material and intangible in nature. Physical features characterize tangible property. Intangible property, on the other hand, does not. Automobiles, literature, clothing, and equipment are examples of tangible personal property. Patents, copyrights, goodwill, and trademarks are examples of intangible property. Stocks, bonds, mutual funds, and money market accounts are also classified as intangible property under tax regulations. Practically every state that taxes intangible property taxes these latter intangibles. If the amount of tax relies on the value of the property, the tax is deductible.

States that levy a tax on tangible personal property often charge property that the owners have registered with the state (e.g. motor vehicles, boats, and aircraft). This permits the tax to be included in the yearly registration cost given to property owners. Individuals in places where the yearly registration charge is dependent on the value of the property can deduct that amount of the fee as an itemized deduction. Any additional fees that are not based on the property's worth are not deductible.

> The Watsons (from above) paid the Department of Motor Vehicles $717 for the annual cost to register their two cars. The fee includes a $50 tag renewal fee. The rest of the fee is based on the value of the car. The Neals deduct $667 ($717 − $50) as personal property tax on Schedule A (line 7).

Other Taxes

Foreign income taxes may be paid by taxpayers having overseas sources of income. Individual taxpayers have two choices for dealing with foreign income taxes paid during the year. To begin, they can claim the taxes as a foreign tax credit. Second, the foreign taxes can be deducted as an itemized deduction. When deducting international taxes, taxpayers put "Foreign income taxes" and the amount on the Schedule A "Other taxes" line.

Interest You Paid

The majority of personal interest is not deductible. Home mortgage interest, points, and investment interest, on the other hand, may qualify as itemized deductions. Interest on student loans, on the other hand, is not an itemized deduction. On Form 1040, page 1, taxpayers deduct student loan interest from their AGI.

Home Mortgage Interest

Taxpayers can deduct interest on eligible home loans, which include debt on the taxpayer's primary dwelling (main home) as well as a second home. A vacation house is considered a second home. Personal dwellings include houses, condominiums, and mobile homes. Boats and motor homes are occasionally accepted. The person paying the interest must also own the home in order to claim the mortgage interest deduction.

Those who own three or more properties can deduct just the mortgage interest paid on their primary residence and one other home of their choice. When allowing others to use a house, to qualify as a second home, the taxpayer must use the property for more than 14 days or more than 10% of the total days it is rented out, whichever is greater. Additionally, the home must be used by the taxpayer or a family member for personal purposes for more than the greater of 14 days or 10% of the total days it is rented out, whichever is greater.

> The Wtasons make mortgage payments on their main home and their vacation home. The interest paid on these properties was $13,215 and $3,220, respectively. The Neals deduct $16,435 ($13,215 + $3,220) as home mortgage interest on Schedule A.

> The Kenyons live most of the year in Dallas, Texas. They vacation in Phoenix, Arizona and Park City, Utah. They own homes in all three locations and have mortgages on all three homes. In the current year, the Kenyons paid interest expense on the Dallas, Phoenix, and Park City mortgages of $6,000, $10,000, and $18,500, respectively. When filing their income tax return, they can deduct the $6,000 interest paid on the loan used to finance their main home (in Dallas). They also can deduct the $18,500 paid on the mortgage of their Park City home. The $10,000 paid on their other vacation home is nondeductible personal interest.

Acquisition Indebtedness

Acquisition indebtedness is one sort of qualified home interest (acquisition debt). This covers money borrowed to buy, develop, or significantly enhance the taxpayer's primary or secondary residence. The limit on acquisition debt has been reduced for tax years 2018 through 2025 due to the Tax Cuts and Jobs Act (TCJA) that was passed in 2017. For tax years 2018 through 2025, only interest paid on acquisition debt up to $750,000 ($375,000 for married taxpayers filing separately) is deductible. This means that the limit on acquisition debt is lower than it was in previous years Nevertheless, there are no interest deduction restrictions for debt acquired prior to October 13, 1987. Yet, a large loan on the primary residence may limit the interest deduction on a second house purchased after this date.

When refinancing the initial loan, certain limitations limit the deduction. If the new loan has a greater balance than the previous loan, the new debt that replaces the old debt is considered acquisition debt. Furthermore, any amount of the excess debt utilized to purchase or upgrade the taxpayer's primary or secondary residence qualifies as acquisition debt. Any leftover additional debt is not purchase debt, but it may be considered home equity debt.

Home Equity Debt

Taxpayers may deduct interest on any loan secured by their residences, subject to certain limitations. Home equity loans and debt consolidation loans are examples of these. Such debt, together with the amount of any acquisition debt, cannot exceed the home's fair market value (FMV). The deduction for interest on home equity loans has been stopped till 2025 as of 2018. Taxpayers are not permitted to deduct interest on home equity loan, regardless of the reason for the debt.

Reporting Home Mortgage Interest

Most taxpayers who have a mortgage receive Form 1098, Mortgage Interest Statement, from their lender. This form informs taxpayers about the amount of mortgage interest paid throughout the fiscal year. Mortgage interest recorded on Form 1098 appears on a separate line on Schedule A from any home mortgage interest paid during the year that was not reported on Form 1098.

Points

Points paid on a mortgage or a refinancing generally must be amortized over the life of the loan, rather than deducted in full in the year that they were paid. However, there are some exceptions to this rule, such as when the loan is used to purchase or improve a main home and the points meet certain criteria.

Under current tax law, points paid on a mortgage or a refinancing may be deductible as interest in the year that they were paid if they meet the following criteria:

1. *The loan is used to purchase or improve the main home of the taxpayer.*
2. *The points are computed as a percentage of the principal amount of the mortgage.*
3. *The points are paid in connection with the mortgage at the time of closing.*
4. *The points are an established business practice in the area where the loan was made.*

The deduction for points may be limited in certain cases, such as when the loan is for more than $750,000, or when the taxpayer's total mortgage debt exceeds a certain amount.

It's also important to note that points paid on a refinancing generally must be deducted over the life of the loan, unless the proceeds are used to improve the main home and certain other criteria are met.

Additionally, points paid on a loan to purchase a second home or an investment property generally must be deducted over the life of the loan. Fees charged for loan services provided by the lender, such as document preparation fees and appraisal fees, are not deductible as points. However, they may be deductible as other types of mortgage interest or as a part of the cost of the home.

When the property is sold or the loan is refinanced, a unique scenario develops. If the property is sold, any unamortized points that were previously deducted must be added back to the taxpayer's income in the year of sale. If the loan is refinanced, the unamortized points from the previous loan, as well as any new points paid as part of the refinancing, are generally deducted over the term of the new loan.

However, for cash basis taxpayers, a portion of the points paid for refinancing a primary residence can be immediately deducted if the funds are used to improve or substantially renovate the home. The remainder of the points can be deducted in equal installments during the loan's duration. Note that this applies only to points paid for the new portion of the loan used for home improvements, not to any points paid on the portion of the loan used to refinance the original mortgage.

Let's say John purchased a home in 2020 and took out a 30-year mortgage for $300,000 at an interest rate of 4%. The lender charged him 2 points (2% of the loan amount) as a loan origination fee, which came out to $6,000. John paid this fee upfront at the closing of the loan.

Because John paid points, he was able to get a lower interest rate of 3.75% on his mortgage. Over the course of the loan, he would save money on interest payments compared to if he had not paid points.

In 2021, John decided to refinance his mortgage to take advantage of lower interest rates. He refinanced with a new lender and took out a new 30-year mortgage for $300,000 at an interest rate of 3.5%. The new lender charged him 1 point (1% of the loan amount) as a loan origination fee, which came out to $3,000. Because John refinanced, he also had to subtract the unamortized points from his old loan.

To calculate the unamortized points, John would first need to figure out how many points he paid and how many years he had left on his old mortgage. He paid 2 points, so the unamortized amount would be $6,000

> (the total points paid) divided by 30 (the number of years on the old mortgage) multiplied by the number of years he had left on the old mortgage. Let's say he had paid his old mortgage for one year before refinancing. The unamortized amount would be $6,000 divided by 30 multiplied by 29 (the number of years left on the old mortgage) which comes out to $5,800.
>
> So when John refinanced his mortgage, he would subtract the $5,800 unamortized points from his old loan and deduct it over the term of his new loan, along with the $3,000 new points he paid on his new loan.

Reporting Points

When points are paid on the acquisition of a primary residence, the amount paid should be recorded on Form 1098. The points are completely deductible in the tax year in which they are paid and are applied to any home mortgage interest recorded on Form 1098. The deductible part of points not reported on Form 1098 is reported on Schedule A's "Points not reported to you on Form 1098" line.

Investment Interests

Investment interest is interest paid on a loan used to purchase or hold taxable investments such as stocks, taxable bonds, empty land, jewels, and artwork. The tax code does not provide deductions for nontaxable income costs. As a result, interest paid on sums borrowed to purchase or hold nontaxable investments (such as municipal bonds) is not deductible.

Certain investments are referred to be "passive" investments. The tax code does not consider interest expenditure on a passive investment to be investment interest. This interest is taken from your tax return in another place. For example, interest expenditure on rental property (a passive investment) should be reported on Schedule E, not Schedule A.

The investment interest limitation restricts investment interest deductions to the amount of the taxpayer's net investment income. Any investment interest that is not deducted due to this restriction may be carried over and used in subsequent years. When carried over to the next year, it behaves exactly like that year's investment interest and is subject to the same limitations.

Taxable interest, non-qualified dividends, and some royalties are examples of investment income. It may also include eligible dividends and gains from investment sales. If the taxpayer elects to tax qualifying dividends and net capital gains at lower tax rates, these sums will not be considered investment income. If the taxpayer chooses to pay the regular tax rates on qualifying dividends and net capital gains, these amounts are considered investment income. This second alternative may enable the taxpayer to deduct more investment interest in the current year.

Net investment income is the excess of the taxpayer's investment income over the amount of investment expenses actually included in the taxpayer's total itemized deductions (i.e., those that exceed the 2% AGI floor). These expenses include fees paid to an investment advisor, safe deposit box rental fees, and the costs of investment publications. Taxpayers file Form 4952, Investment Interest, to support their investment interest deduction on Schedule A.

> Joel borrows $30,000 to purchase taxable investments. He pays $2,800 of interest on the loan during the year. Joel is in the 31% tax bracket. During the year his investments produce $1,600 in taxable interest, $600 in qualified dividends, $240 in nonqualified dividends, and $1,600 in net capital gains. The $1,840 of taxable interest and nonqualified dividends counts as investment income. However, the $2,200 of qualified dividends and net capital gains only counts as investment income if Joel elects to tax these amounts at his normal (31%) tax rate.
>
> Joel's options regarding the investment interest are as follows. First, he can choose to tax the $2,200 of qualified dividends and net capital gains at the lower 15% tax rate. This will result in his investment interest expense being limited to his $1,840 of investment income. He would carry over the $960 excess ($2,800 − $1,840) to the next tax year. Joel's second option is to elect to tax $960 of the qualified dividends and net capital gains at the 31% tax rate. If he does this, then his investment income will increase to $2,800 ($1,840 + $960). This will allow him to deduct the entire $2,800 of investment interest in the current year. He will then be allowed to tax the remaining $1,240 of qualified dividends and net capital gains ($2,200 − $960) at the lower 15% tax rate.

Gifts to Charity

People can deduct both cash and noncash property donated to a qualifying charity as an itemized deduction. The amount that may be deducted in any given year is determined by the taxpayer's AGI.

The ceiling for monetary gifts made in tax years beginning after 2017 is 60% of the taxpayer's AGI.

The standard maximum for noncash property gifts is 30% of AGI, however it may be lower for particular types of property. Any AGI-restricted deductions roll over to the next five tax years.

Gifts by Cash or Check
Donations must be given to recognized charity organizations in order to be tax deductible. To deduct contributions to other countries for disaster relief and other reasons, taxpayers must make the donation to a qualified nonprofit organization in the United States.

The standard mileage rate for charitable use of a vehicle is currently $.14 per mile in 2023. This rate is set by the IRS annually. However, taxpayers can also choose to deduct the actual expenses of operating their vehicle for charitable purposes, such as gas, oil, repairs, and insurance, instead of using the standard mileage rate. In this case, the taxpayer should keep detailed records of their expenses and the miles driven for charitable purposes. Vehicle expenditures are considered financial gifts. Donations are generally deductible in the year in which they are made, regardless of whether the taxpayer utilizes the cash or accrual approach. Receipts must be kept by taxpayers to support their deduction. If the charity provided the taxpayer with any items or services in exchange for their donation, the amount of the deduction must be reduced by the value of what the taxpayer got.

> The Watsonss paid $400 a plate for a YMCA benefit
> and made a cash donation of $3,000 at the banquet. The
> YMCA's cost for the dinner was $20 per person. The
> Watsons could have bought the same two meals at a
> bistro for $75. The charitable contribution deduction is
> $3,725, the difference between the amount donated and
> the value of the dinner ($3,000 cash donation + $800
> meals − $75 value). The Watsons do not take the
> YMCA's cost into account. They enter $3,725 on the
> "Gifts by cash or check" line on Schedule A.

Taxpayers may only deduct gifts made to qualified
non-profit organizations. All other gifts are not
deductible. Handouts to needy people may be
generous, but they are not deductible.

> Qualified charities are nonprofit organizations that are
> exempt from tax under Section 501(c)(3) of the Internal
> Revenue Code. They include organizations that operate
> solely for religious, scientific, charitable, literary, or
> educational purposes. They also include organizations
> that promote the arts or to prevent cruelty to children or
> animals. This is only a partial list of the types of
> organizations that qualify as 501(c)(3) organizations. A
> complete list of qualified charities can be found on the
> IRS website.

Contributions in exchange for the right to purchase Colligate Athletic Tickets

Some gifts to a college or university are subject to a
particular restriction. When a taxpayer's donation
allows the taxpayer to purchase tickets to sporting
events, 80% of the gift is deemed a charitable
contribution. The remaining 20% is a nondeductible
right to purchase the tickets.

> Dwayne donates $1,000 to his alma mater. His gift allows him to buy season tickets to the university's football and basketball games. The tax law treats $800 ($1,000 × 80%) as a charitable contribution. The rest ($200) is treated as a nondeductible payment for the right to purchase athletic tickets.

Non-Cash Gifts

Donations of property that fall into one of two categories are subject to special rules: (1) regular income property (all property kept for one year or less) or (2) capital gain property retained for more than one year. Real estate, tangible personal property, and intangible personal property can all be donated in both categories.

Tangible personal property includes the majority of tangible property owned by a taxpayer that is not real estate. Clothing, toys, furniture, appliances, and books are common things donated under this category. The FMV of these things is usually less than the taxpayer's base. The FMV of home items and apparel is the worth in a thrift store or garage sale. The "blue book" value of a car is a popular source of valuation.

Stocks, bonds, and mutual funds are the most typically gifted intangible assets. The majority of these assets are extensively traded, and their FMV is simple to calculate. The deduction for noncash gifts is generally equivalent to the fair market value of the property at the time of giving. When the FMV is less than the taxpayer's basis (investment) in the property, this is true. When the FMV exceeds the basis, the amount of the deduction is determined by whether the item is (1) regular income property or long-term capital gain property and (2) how the charity utilizes the property.

As of 2021, the threshold for filing Form 8283 for noncash charitable donations has increased to $5,000. Taxpayers must fill out Section A of Form 8283 for noncash donations totaling between $500 and $5,000, and they must fill out both Sections A and B for noncash donations exceeding $5,000. Additionally, the receipt from the qualified organization must include a description of any goods or services provided in exchange for the donation, as well as a statement indicating whether any goods or services were provided at a value greater than the fair market value of the donation.

Note: Taxpayers who donate vehicles to charities that then sell the vehicles can only deduct what the charity gets from the sale. The charity may incur penalties if it does not report the sales price to both the donor and the IRS.

> The Watsons make several non-cash donations during the year. Even though the amounts paid for the donated items were far greater than their value at the time of the donations, their deduction is limited to the FMV of the donated items. The Watsons got receipts from the charities for each of their donations, and use thrift store value to arrive at their $720 deduction.

Ordinary Income Property
Conventional income property is defined as property that, if sold, would generate income subject to regular (ordinary) taxation. It comprises assets such as business inventories and investments held for less than a year. When a taxpayer contributes conventional income property, the value

of the donation is limited by the taxpayer's basis (investment) in the property. This is usually the amount paid by the taxpayer for the property. As a result, there is no deduction for the value of personal services provided to a charity.

> Alejandro Gomez built a bookcase and donated it to the local public high school. The bookcase was appraised at $800. The Gomez spent $125 on materials. They deduct only the $125 cost of materials, as the bookcase would be ordinary income property if they had sold it. They receive no deduction for the value of Alejandro's time in constructing the bookcase.

Capital Gain Property

Capital gain property is defined as certain valued assets kept for more than a year that, if sold, would result in long-term capital gain. Stocks, bonds, and real estate are all included in this category. It also comprises the majority of an individual's investments and personal items. The value of the gift is determined by the FMV at the time of donation. To determine the worth, taxpayers can get written appraisals or stock market quotes. When the FMV of an item exceeds the taxpayer's basis, taxpayers who donate to eligible charity receive a tax break. The donor chooses not to record the higher value as income. In addition to avoiding paying taxes on the asset's appreciation, the donor is able to deduct the greater FMV amount.

The Watsons donated shares of IBM stock to their church. They paid $2,000 for the stock many years ago. On the date of the donation, the stock was worth $3,500. The Watsons' deduction for noncash contributions total $4,220 ($720 from earlier example + $3,500 FMV of the stock). Since this amount exceeds $500, the Watsons complete Form 8283 to provide details of their noncash donations. They attach Form 8283 to their tax return and enter $4,220 on the "Other than cash or check" line on Schedule A.

The Code enables taxpayers to deduct just their basis in appreciated tangible personal property when it is not utilized directly for the charity's tax-exempt purpose. This regulation only applies to appreciated tangible personal property donations. As a result, the decreased deduction does not apply to donations of capital gain property that is either intangible or real estate.

Ray, an art collector, donates a painting worth $25,000 to the local hospital. Ray paid $3,000 for the painting years ago. The painting is tangible personal property held long-term. Thus, it is capital gain property. However, since the hospital cannot use the painting in relation to its exempt purpose (treating patients), Ray's charitable deduction is limited to $3,000.

In a different scenario, Ray donates the painting to a local art museum. Since the painting will be put to use in the museum's tax-exempt purpose, Ray can deduct the full $25,000 FMV of the painting.

Same facts as above except that Ray purchased the painting nine months earlier. Since the painting was not held for more than one year at the time it was donated, if it had been sold it would have produced short-term capital gain taxed at Ray's regular (ordinary) tax rate. Thus, the painting is ordinary income property. The Code limits the deduction of such property to Ray's $3,000 basis.

Same facts as above, except that the donated property was stock in a corporation. Stock is intangible property and Ray held it for more than one year prior to donating it. Thus, the stock is capital gain property, and the Code allows Ray to deduct the $25,000 FMV of the stock.

Same facts as in Example 28, except that the property donated was land held as an investment. Since land is real property that Ray held it for more than one year, it is capital gain property and Ray deducts the $25,000 FMV of the land.

Same facts as in Example 28, except that Ray paid $25,000 for the painting and at the time it was donated, it was worth $3,000. Since the painting declined in value since Ray bought it, it is not capital gain (appreciated) property. The general rule allows Ray to deduct the ($3,000) FMV of the property.

Non Deductible Gifts

Before making a donation, taxpayers should confirm if the charity is a 501(c)(3) organization. This information is available on the IRS website. Several fund-raising organizations appear to be certified charity but are not. Contributions to qualifying organizations' lobbying or political action groups may not be deductible. Other non-deductible contributions include dues to clubs or lodges and tuition paid to private or religious schools. Also, the purchase of raffle tickets is not tax deductible.

Limitations

The Tax Cuts and Jobs Act of 2017 (TCJA) made some changes to the charitable contribution deduction rules.

Under current law, the deduction for cash contributions to public charities is limited to 60% of the taxpayer's adjusted gross income (AGI) for the year. For donations of appreciated property, such as stocks or real estate, the limit is generally 30% of AGI. If the taxpayer's total deductions for noncash contributions during the year exceed $500, they must still complete Form 8283.

However, it's important to note that the TCJA also nearly doubled the standard deduction and limited the state and local tax deduction to $10,000, which significantly reduced the number of taxpayers who itemize deductions, including charitable contributions. To help increase charitable giving, the CARES Act of 2020 temporarily increased the deduction limit for cash contributions to public charities to 100% of AGI for taxpayers who itemize their deductions. This provision has since expired, but there are still some other ways to maximize charitable giving deductions, such as donor-advised funds and qualified charitable distributions from IRAs for taxpayers over age 70½.

Taxpayers can avoid the 30% AGI limit on the contribution of appreciated capital gain property by contributing the property to a public charity, rather than a private foundation. If the donation is made to a public charity, the deduction limit is increased to 50% of AGI. When taxpayers contribute capital gain property to private nonoperating foundations, the deduction is limited to 30% of AGI, not 20%.

For cash contributions, the deduction limit is increased to 60% of AGI for the tax years 2020 and 2021, as part of the Coronavirus Aid, Relief, and Economic Security (CARES) Act. This increased limit only applies to cash contributions made to public charities. For noncash contributions, the threshold for filing Form 8283 has increased from $500 to $5,000, as part of the Tax Cuts and Jobs Act (TCJA) of 2017.

It's also worth noting that there are some other rules and limitations that apply to charitable contributions, depending on the type of property donated and the nature of the organization receiving the donation. Taxpayers should consult the IRS website or a tax professional for more information.

Let's say John has an AGI of $100,000 in 2022 and he wants to make charitable donations throughout the year. He contributes $10,000 in cash to a public charity and $15,000 worth of appreciated stock to a private foundation. The fair market value of the stock is $15,000 and John's cost basis in the stock is $5,000.

For the cash donation to the public charity, John can deduct up to 50% of his AGI, which is $50,000. Since he donated $10,000, he can fully deduct the donation.

For the donation of appreciated stock to the private foundation, John's deduction is limited to 30% of his AGI, which is $30,000. However, if he reduces the amount of the donation to his cost basis, the limit increases to 50% of his AGI, which is $50,000. So, if John decides to reduce his donation of stock to his cost basis of $5,000, he can fully deduct the $5,000 and carry over the remaining $10,000 to the next year.

Reporting Carryovers

The AGI restrictions of 50%, 30%, and 20% can occasionally diminish a taxpayer's contribution deduction. Unused contributions can be carried forward for up to five years by taxpayers. Contributions are subject to the same 50%, 30%, and 20% AGI restrictions when carried forward. Unused contributions subject to the 30% AGI restriction in 20x1 are, for example, subject to the same 30% AGI limit when carried over to 20x2. On Schedule A, taxpayers declare the deductible amount of contributions carried over from a previous tax year on the "Carryover from preceding year" line.

Casualty and Theft Loss

People may deduct losses incurred when their personal items are stolen or destroyed in a disaster. They calculate each casualty (or theft) loss as the smaller of (i) the difference in FMV before and after the casualty (or theft) or (ii) the property's basis.

This sum is reduced first by any insurance or other reimbursements received, and then by $100 per event (not per item). The net loss from each casualty event that happens during the year is then totaled by the taxpayers. They deduct 10% of AGI from this total. Just the remainder is deductible.

Loans taken out to compensate losses are not considered reimbursements. When a person has insurance but chooses not to disclose an occurrence in order to avoid raising insurance premiums, no personal casualty loss deduction is made for the amount of insurance benefits foregone.

Many of these limitations make it difficult to deduct losses from personal injuries. Personal casualty deductions are rarely made unless there is a significant uninsured calamity. Smaller injuries often result in losses less than 10% of AGI and no tax advantages. The casualty loss deduction is calculated on Form 4684, Casualties and Thefts, and the net loss in excess of 10% of AGI is entered on Schedule A. If more than one casualty occurs throughout the year, taxpayers must complete a separate Form 4684 for each incident.

Drew wrecked his personal automobile that originally cost $30,000. This was his only casualty for the year. The vehicle had a FMV of $25,855 before the accident. The estimated FMV after the accident was $1,000, resulting in a $24,855 change in value ($25,855 − $1,000). Drew collected $16,355 of insurance proceeds. His AGI of $52,090 reduces the casualty loss deduction to $3,191.

Lesser of (i) $24,855 change in FMV or (ii) $30,000 basis	$24,855
Less insurance proceeds	- 16,355
Less $100 reduction	- 100
Less 10% of AGI	- 5,209
Net casualty loss deduction, not less than $0	$ 3,191

Taxpayers may be eligible to deduct from their gross income payments received to offset increased living expenses incurred as a result of a disaster. Such sums are not taxed if they reimburse the taxpayer for a temporary rise in living expenses. Reimbursements in excess of real costs, as well as reimbursements for regular expenses, are taxed. While these reimbursements are frequently connected with casualties, they have no effect on the casualty loss deduction.

> A casualty damages a couple's home. While repairing the home, the couple lives in another house, costing them $3,500 per month. The couple's normal living expenses before the storm were $1,500 per month. They continue to pay all of their normal living expenses in addition to the $3,500 each month. The insurance company reimburses the couple $4,000 per month. They include $500 per month in gross income for the reimbursement they receive in excess of the $3,500 increase in living expenses.

Casualty Events

A casualty is defined by the IRS as a sudden, unexpected, or unusual incident. Accidents, fires, storms, earthquakes, floods, hurricanes, thefts, and other calamities are examples of events that cause casualty losses. Many annoying incidents, while costly and uncomfortable, may not qualify as casualties because they are not abrupt, unexpected, or exceptional. Long-term termite or moth damage, plant disease, property value decline owing to a landslide on a nearby lot, or loss of a diamond ring thrown into a sewer are some instances. There is no deduction for objects intentionally destroyed or damaged due to purposeful negligence.

Moreover, deductions are only permitted for damage to the taxpayer's own property. As a result, if a motorist hits and damages a neighbor's fence, the cost of restoring the neighbor's fence cannot be deducted on the driver's tax return as a casualty loss.

Proof

A casualty is not created simply by the loss of an object. The taxpayer must demonstrate that a theft, accident, or tragedy occurred. Taxpayers should report any loss to the police or another government agency so that they may obtain a written report for their records. The amount of the casualty loss must also be determined by the taxpayer.

Before and after photos might assist demonstrate the degree of the damage. Objective valuations of the property before and after the occurrence offer proof of the loss. The IRS will usually take the cost of repairing the property as the loss amount. Nevertheless, if the repairs restore the property to a better state and a greater worth than before the loss, the cost of repairs cannot be utilised.

Year of Deduction

A casualty loss deduction is generally allowed only in the year in which the casualty occurs. The taxpayer deducts a theft loss in the year the theft is discovered. The taxpayer may, however, decide to deduct a loss incurred in a federally declared disaster region in the year of the catastrophe or the prior tax year. This unique regulation allows taxpayers to get disaster-related tax refunds sooner.

Reduction in Itemized Deductions for Higher-Income Taxpayers

Higher-income taxpayers must reduce their total itemized deductions by up to 3% of AGI in excess of a specified threshold, with the threshold amounts varying by filing status. The specific threshold amounts for tax year 2022 are:

Married filing jointly (MFJ) and qualifying widow(er): $318,800
Head of household (HOH): $293,250
Single: $269,250
Married filing separately (MFS): $159,400

However, the limitation on itemized deductions has been adjusted for inflation and is now calculated as 80% of all itemized deductions other than medical and dental expenses, investment interest expenses, casualty or theft losses, and gambling losses. This limitation applies to taxpayers with income above a certain threshold, which for tax year 2022 is $334,000 for married taxpayers filing jointly and $167,000 for all other taxpayers.

Let's say that in 2022, John and Jane are married filing jointly and have an AGI of $350,000. They have $40,000 in state and local taxes, $20,000 in mortgage interest, and $10,000 in charitable contributions. The threshold for reducing itemized deductions for MFJ filers in 2022 is $305,050.

To calculate the reduction, John and Jane first subtract the threshold amount from their AGI: $350,000 - $305,050 = $44,950. Then they multiply that amount by 3%: $44,950 x 0.03 = $1,348.50. This is the amount by which they must reduce their itemized deductions.

Next, they add up all of their itemized deductions: $40,000 + $20,000 + $10,000 = $70,000. They multiply that amount by 80%: $70,000 x 0.8 = $56,000. Finally, they subtract the reduction amount: $56,000 - $1,348.50 = $54,651.50. This is the total amount of itemized deductions they can claim on their tax return.

Without the reduction, John and Jane's itemized deductions would have been $70,000. However, because their AGI exceeds the threshold, they are required to reduce their itemized deductions by $1,348.50.

Chapter 6

Rental Activities

Many people generate revenue from property they own in addition to income from their work. Taxpayers who own stocks, for example, frequently get dividend income. Bondholders gain interest income as well. Taxpayers can also generate money by renting out their own property. This chapter focuses on the revenue and expenditures generated by rental operations. Rental income and costs are reported on Form E, Supplementary Income and Loss. Nevertheless, if rental expenditures exceed rental revenue, the vacation home rules, at-risk rules, or passive loss rules may restrict the losses that can be deducted on Form 1040. The chapter starts with a look of rental revenue and costs. The emphasis then changes to areas of tax law that may limit deductions for rental losses.

Rental Incomes and Expenses

Although taxpayers can rent both personal and real property, the tax implications of owning residential rental property are the subject of this chapter. Residential rental property is defined as rental property that generates at least 80% of its revenue from the renting as dwelling units. A housing unit is real estate that includes basic living accommodations such as a kitchen, sleeping quarters, and bathroom facilities. Houses, apartments, condominiums, mobile homes, motor homes, yachts, and boats are all examples of habitation units. Hotels, motels, and other similar enterprises do not qualify as residential units.

Rental Income

Rental revenue comprises money received by taxpayers for letting others to use or occupy their property. Rent payments are usually made in cash. When a tenant delivers services in return for the use of the taxpayer's property, however, rental income includes the value of those services. Rental income comprises payments made by tenants to end a lease. It also covers the cost of modifications made by a renter to the taxpayer's property in lieu of rent.

> Stef rents property he owns to a tenant for $500 a month. In November the tenant installs a ceiling fan valued at $100. Stef reduces the tenant's December rent by $100. Stef's rental income equals $6,000 ($500 × 11 months + $400 for December + $100 improvement in lieu of rent). Stef then capitalizes and depreciates the ceiling fan.

Rental income is reported by cash basis taxpayers in the year it is received, even if it pertains to a former or future tax year. Rental income is typically reported in the year it is payable to accrual basis taxpayers, however rent paid in advance must be reported in the year it is received. As a result, if a taxpayer received $600 from a tenant for January 20x2 rent on December 26, 20x1, the $600 would be recorded as rental revenue in 20x1 under both the cash and accrual methods. When a security deposit reflects the tenant's final rent payment, it is considered rent paid in advance. If the taxpayer plans to return the deposit at the conclusion of the lease, it is not regarded rent collected in advance. However, if the renter forfeits any portion of the deposit in a subsequent year (for example, to meet late fees), the amount forfeited is taxable income to the taxpayer in the year the tenant forfeits it.

> Donna enters into a 5-year lease to rent property she owns. On July 1, 20x1, she receives $6,000 for the first year's rent and $6,000 of rent in advance for the final year of the lease. Donna also receives a $1,000 security deposit that she intends to return to the tenant at the end of the lease. Her 20x1 rental income equals $12,000, regardless of whether she uses the cash or accrual method of accounting.

Rental Expenses

All typical expenditures linked to the rental property can be deducted by taxpayers from rental revenue. Advertising, cleaning, utilities, real estate taxes, mortgage interest, insurance premiums, management fees, and essential travel and transportation are all examples of frequent rental expenditures. Repairs, upkeep, and depreciation are examples of additional rental costs. Accrual basis taxpayers deduct expenses in the year they obtain services or use assets. Except for anticipated expenditures, which are amortized across the periods benefited, cash basis taxpayers deduct rental expenses in the year they are paid.

Maintenance and Repairs

Repairs and upkeep maintain the rental property in working order. Taxpayers can deduct the price of rental property repairs and upkeep as a rental expenditure. Painting the property (inside and out), repairing gutters or leaks, and replacing broken windows are all examples of repairs. Repairs are small expenses that should not be confused with renovations that increase the value of the rental property or extend its useful life. Adding a bathroom, paving a driveway, installing new cabinetry, or repairing the roof are all examples of rental property improvements. The taxpayer's investment (basis) in the rental property grows as a result of the improvements. Improvements are not deductible as a rental expenditure by taxpayers. Instead, they use the depreciation procedures indicated below to recoup the cost of upgrades.

Depreciation
Residential real estate placed in operation after 1986 is depreciated by taxpayers using the straight-line method over 27.5 years (MACRS) or 40 years (ADS). Land is not depreciated. Taxpayers can also deduct furniture utilized in a rental real estate operation using MACRS or ADS. Furniture, appliances, and flooring are all included. Section 179 cannot be used to purchase rental property. Nevertheless, bonus depreciation is available on new rental furniture placed in service during a bonus depreciation year in the first year. Rental furniture are 5-year property if MACRS is employed. Rental furniture have a 9-year recovery time if ADS is chosen.

However, it is important to note that bonus depreciation is set to gradually phase out over the next several years. For property placed in service in 2023, the bonus depreciation rate will be 60%, in 2024 it will be 40%, and in 2025 it will be 20% before phasing out completely in 2026, unless there are legislative changes.

Duncan spends $15,000 to replace the roof and $3,000 to repaint the exterior of an apartment building he owns. Duncan can deduct the $3,000 spent on repairs from rental income in the current year. Duncan adds the $15,000 of improvements to his basis in the apartment building and depreciates this amount over 27.5 years under MACRS or 40 years under ADS.

Special Rules When Only One Part of The Apartment Is Rented

The guidelines just mentioned presuppose that the rental property is solely or primarily used by rent-paying renters. Occasionally an individual rents only a portion of a property, such as when the owner of a duplex rents one apartment while living in the other. In such cases, the taxpayer must divide his or her costs between rental and personal usage. The taxpayer then deducts the rental part of each cost from rental income and can itemize the personal component of mortgage interest and real estate taxes.

Certain costs are simple to divide between rental and personal usage. Taxpayers, for example, can completely deduct the cost of repairs conducted on rental units but cannot deduct the cost of repairs performed on their own personal apartments. Some costs, like as real estate taxes and depreciation, are more difficult to separate between rental and personal usage. Taxpayers can apportion these costs between the two uses using any acceptable way. The number of rooms or the proportional square footage are two popular approaches for distributing these costs.

Marvin rents one room in his home. The area of the rented room is 140 square feet. The area of the entire home is 1,400 square feet. Marvin deducts against rental income 10% (140/1,400) of the expenses related to the home during the year. Thus, if Marvin's real estate taxes are $2,000, he can deduct $200 against rental income and the rest ($1,800) as an itemized deduction.

Transforming A Personal Home Into A Rental Property

When a taxpayer converts a personal residence to rental property, the costs from the conversion year must be divided between the two uses. The rental period begins when the property is initially made available for rent. The rental share of these expenditures is deducted by taxpayers from rental revenue. As itemized deductions, they can deduct the personal component of mortgage interest and real estate taxes.

In September, Lola moved out of her home. Lola listed her home for rent on October 1, and on November 1, she entered into a 2-year lease. Lola can deduct 25% (October–December) of the annual expenses (real estate taxes, insurance, depreciation) against the rental income she receives during the year. She also can deduct any other expenses (mortgage interest, utilities, etc.) allocated to the last three months of the year. Lola can deduct the personal portion (the other 75%) of the interest and taxes as itemized deductions.

Vacation Home Rental

When taxpayers rent out their residences for part of the year while personally using the property the rest of the year, certain regulations apply. The tax treatment of this sort of rental activity is determined by the number of rental and personal days in the calendar year.

Property rented for less than 15 days
Individual taxpayers who rent their primary residence or vacation property for less than 15 days during the year do not declare rental revenue and do not deduct rental expenditures. Home mortgage interest (but only for the taxpayer's primary or secondary residence), real estate taxes, and casualty losses, on the other hand, may be claimed as itemized deductions.

Marcus rents his vacation home for 12 days during the year and personally uses it for 80 days. The rest of the year the home sits vacant. Benton collects rents of $3,000 and incurs the following expenses.

Home mortgage interest	$ 6,000
Real estate taxes	1,800
Utilities	400
Depreciation	2,000
Total expenses	$10,200

Since Marcus rents the property for less than 15 days, he does not report the $3,000 of rental income.

Marcus can deduct as itemized deductions the $6,000 of home mortgage interest (as his second home) and the $1,800 of real estate taxes.

Property rented for more than 14 days

Rental income is reported on personal tax returns by taxpayers who rent their primary residence or vacation property for more than 14 days during the year. Rental-related expenses (such as advertising or commissions) can be deducted from rental revenue. All other costs must be divided equally between rental and personal usage. The rental component of these expenditures can subsequently be deducted by taxpayers.

Taxpayers are required by the Internal Revenue Code (Code) to distribute costs other than interest, taxes, and casualty losses based on the number of days the property is used during the year. To calculate the rental part of expenditures such as utilities, repairs, and depreciation, taxpayers multiplied the expense by the ratio of days rented at fair rental value to days used throughout the year.

Percent allocated to rental activity = Number of days rented at fair rental price during the year/Number of days used during the year

The Code makes no mention of dividing interest, taxes, and casualty losses between rental and personal usage. The IRS recommends that taxpayers use the same technique they use to apportion other costs in IRS Publication 527. Yet, the courts have permitted interest and taxes to be calculated based on the number of days rented rather than the number of days in the year. For the purposes of this chapter, all expenditures are allocated between rental and personal usage using the same ratio (days rented/days utilized).

Jon rents out his vacation home for 120 days during the year. He personally uses it for 80 days. Jon collects rents of $12,000 and incurs the following expenses.

Home mortgage interest	$8,000
Real estate taxes	2,500
Utilities	800
Depreciation	3,000
Total expenses	14,300

Jon allocates 60% of the expenses (120 rental days/200 total days used during the year) to rental use. He deducts $8,580 ($14,300 × 60%) as rental expense.

Jon can deduct the rest of the real estate taxes ($2,500 × 40% = $1,000) as an itemized deduction. He may be able to deduct the rest of the home mortgage interest ($8,000 × 40% = $3,200) if the home is selected as Jon's second home.

A rental day is any day where the taxpayer rents the property for a reasonable rent, even if it is to a friend or relative. Days when the property is advertised for rent but not rented do not qualify as days rented at a reasonable rental price.

What Is a Fair Rental Price?

A fair rental price is the amount of rent that an unrelated person would be willing to pay to use the property. If the rent charged is substantially less than the rents received on similar properties, it might not be considered a fair rental price. The following questions can be used to determine whether two properties are similar: **Are the properties used for the same purpose? Are the properties about the same size? Are the properties in about the same condition? Do the properties have similar furnishings? Are the properties in similar locations?** Generally, answering "No" to any of these questions means that the two properties are not similar

Costs for Certain Holiday Houses are Restricted

When a property is classified as a "residence," rental expenditures are only deducted to the amount of rental revenue. Disallowed costs are carried over to offset rental revenue in subsequent tax years. A vacation house is considered a dwelling if the number of personal days exceeds the larger of (i) 14 days or (ii) 10% of the days rented at fair rental.

Consequently, the property is considered a dwelling if the taxpayer's personal days exceed both (i) 14 days and (ii) 10% of the number of days rented at fair rate. If the property is designated as the taxpayer's second home and is classified as a dwelling, the personal component of the mortgage interest can be claimed as an itemized deduction. The personal component of the interest cannot be deducted if the property does not qualify as a dwelling.

It is critical to understand what days constitute as personal days in order to correctly evaluate whether the taxpayer's house qualifies as a dwelling. Days when the taxpayer provides use of the property to a charitable organization are considered personal usage. Personal usage also covers days when the property is utilized by the following people:

1. The owner, unless the owner is repairing or maintaining the property full-time.
2. A member of the owner's family, unless the family member pays a fair rental payment and utilizes the property as his or her primary residence. Siblings (brothers and sisters), ancestors (parents, grandparents, etc.), and lineal descendants

(children, grandchildren, etc.) are examples of family members.

3. Someone has a reciprocal arrangement allowing the owner to utilize another residential unit (e.g., time shares).

4. Someone who pays less than the appropriate rate for the use of the property.

Arya owns a house that she rents to her son. The son pays a fair rental price to use the house as his main home. Arya does not consider the son's use of the house personal days since the son is using the house as his main home and paying fair rental.

Jesse and Ana Lewis own a vacation home that they personally use 24 days during the year. During part of the year, the following occupants used the home. The home was vacant during the rest of the year. Fair rental price is $125 a night.

Occupant	Number of Days
Ana's parents, who pay no rent	32
Friends of the Lindens, who paid rent of $2,000	40
Jesse's brother, who paid rent of $875	7
Unrelated persons, who paid rent of $7,500	60

The 60 days the home was used by unrelated persons are not personal days, since the tenants paid fair rental. Although Jesse's brother paid fair rental, his seven days count as personal days since he is a family member and the home was not used as his main home. The parents did not pay fair rental, nor did they use the home as their main home. Thus, their 32 days count as personal days. The 40 days that the home is used by the Lewis' friends count as personal days since they did not pay fair rental price to use the home. The Lewis' total personal days equal 103 (24 + 32 + 40 + 7). Since the 103 personal days exceed both 14 days and 6.7 days (10% of the 67 days that the Lindens received a fair rental price), the vacation home qualifies as a residence. Thus, rental expenses will be limited to rental income.

> Same facts as above, except that five of the days the Lewis spent at the vacation home were spent making repairs to the property. These five days no longer count as personal days. The Lewis' personal days are reduced to 98 (103 − 5). However, the home still qualifies as a residence.

> David rents his vacation home for 200 days during the year. On 40 of the 200 days, David's sister paid fair rental to use the house. The other 160 days also were rented at fair rental. David treats the days his sister rents the house as personal days, since she does not use the house as her main home. The 40 personal days exceed the greater of 14 days or 10% of the 200 days rented at a fair rental price. Thus, the vacation home qualifies as a residence. Accordingly, even though 100% of the rental expenses are deductible (since all 200 days the home was used during the year were rented at a fair rental price), David can only deduct the rental expenses to the extent of rental income.

If the rental property qualifies as a residence and the taxpayer's rental expenses exceed rental income, the taxpayer deducts the expenses against the rental income in the following order:

1. Home mortgage interest, real estate taxes, casualty and theft losses, and rental expenses not directly related to the rental property (management fees, advertising, etc.)
2. All other rental expenses other than depreciation on the rental property
3. Depreciation of the rental property

NOTE: *When renting out a vacation home, the owner's personal use of the property will determine whether the limitation rules apply. These rules* *cannot take effect until the owner's personal days exceed 14. Thus, to avoid having the tax law limit the deduction for rental expenses, owners might consider limiting their personal usage of the home to two weeks a year.*

Marilyn rents her vacation home at a fair rental price to an unrelated party for 35 days during the year. Marilyn personally uses the home for 15 days. The property is not used during any other time. During the year, Marilyn collects $6,000 in rents and has the following expenses:

Home mortgage interest $ 6,000
Real estate taxes 1,500
Utilities 300
Depreciation 3,000
Total expenses $10,800

Marilyn allocates 70% (35 rental days/50 total days used) of the expenses to the rental use. The rental portion of the expenses related to the home equals $7,560 ($10,800 × 70%). Because Marilyn's personal use (15 days) exceeds the greater of (i) 14 days or (ii) 10% of the days rented at fair rental (35 × 10% = 3.5), the vacation home is treated as a residence.

Thus, Marilyn's rental expenses cannot exceed rental income. Marilyn deducts the rental expenses in the following order:

Rental income	$6,000
Less rental portion of interest and taxes ($7,500×70%)	-(5,250)
Rental income left to cover rent expenses other than interest and taxes	$750
Less rent expenses other than depreciation ($300 × 70%)	-(210)
Rental income left to cover depreciation expense	$ 540
Less depreciation ($3,000 × 70% = $2,100)	-(540)
Net rental income	$ 0

Marilyn can deduct only $540 of the $2,100 of depreciation allocated to rental use. Marilyn carries over the disallowed depreciation of $1,560 ($2,100 − $540) to the next year. She adds this amount to next year's depreciation expense. Marilyn deducts the $450 personal portion of the real estate taxes ($1,500 × 30%) as an itemized deduction. Since the home qualifies as a residence, Marilyn can select the vacation home as her second home and deduct the $1,800 ($6,000 × 30%) personal portion of the home mortgage interest as an itemized deduction.

NOTE: Whenever a vacation house is rented out, the owner's personal use of the property determines whether the limitation regulations apply. These regulations will not be implemented until the owner's personal days surpass 14. To avoid having the tax rules limit the deduction for rental expenditures, owners may choose to limit their personal use of the residence to two weeks each year.

Reporting Rental Activities Schedule E

Schedule E (Form 1040), Supplemental Income and Loss, is used by taxpayers to record rental income and costs. Taxpayers indicate the address for each property in Part I (line 1).

Section I (line 2) requires taxpayers to enter the number of fair rental days and personal usage days. These figures are used to establish if the property is suitable for living in. Rental revenue and costs used in calculating total income or loss from rental activity are also reported by taxpayers in Part I.

SCHEDULE E
(Form 1040 or 1040-SR)

Department of the Treasury
Internal Revenue Service (99)

Supplemental Income and Loss
(From rental real estate, royalties, partnerships, S corporations, estates, trusts, REMICs, etc.)

► Attach to Form 1040, 1040-SR, 1040-NR, or 1041.
► Go to www.irs.gov/ScheduleE for instructions and the latest information.

OMB No. 1545-0074

2019

Attachment Sequence No. 13

Name(s) shown on return

Your social security number

Part I Income or Loss From Rental Real Estate and Royalties Note: If you are in the business of renting personal property, use Schedule C (see instructions). If you are an individual, report farm rental income or loss from Form 4835 on page 2, line 40.

A Did you make any payments in 2019 that would require you to file Form(s) 1099? (see instructions) . . . . . ☐ Yes ☐ No
B If "Yes," did you or will you file required Forms 1099? . . . . ☐ Yes ☐ No

1a Physical address of each property (street, city, state, ZIP code)
A
B
C

1b	Type of Property (from list below)	2 For each rental real estate property listed above, report the number of fair rental and personal use days. Check the QJV box only if you meet the requirements to file as a qualified joint venture. See instructions.		Fair Rental Days	Personal Use Days	QJV
A		A				☐
B		B				☐
C		C				☐

Type of Property:
1 Single Family Residence   3 Vacation/Short-Term Rental 5 Land   7 Self-Rental
2 Multi-Family Residence   4 Commercial   6 Royalties   8 Other (describe)

Income:	Properties:		A	B	C
3 Rents received	3				
4 Royalties received	4				
Expenses:					
5 Advertising	5				
6 Auto and travel (see instructions) . .	6				
7 Cleaning and maintenance	7				
8 Commissions	8				
9 Insurance	9				
10 Legal and other professional fees . .	10				
11 Management fees	11				
12 Mortgage interest paid to banks, etc. (see instructions)	12				
13 Other interest	13				
14 Repairs	14				
15 Supplies	15				
16 Taxes	16				
17 Utilities	17				
18 Depreciation expense or depletion . .	18				
19 Other (list) ►	19				
20 Total expenses. Add lines 5 through 19	20				
21 Subtract line 20 from line 3 (rents) and/or 4 (royalties). If result is a (loss), see instructions to find out if you must file Form 6198.	21				
22 Deductible rental real estate loss after limitation, if any, on Form 8582 (see instructions) . .	22	(	)	( )	( )

23a Total of all amounts reported on line 3 for all rental properties . . .	23a		
b Total of all amounts reported on line 4 for all royalty properties . . .	23b		
c Total of all amounts reported on line 12 for all properties	23c		
d Total of all amounts reported on line 18 for all properties	23d		
e Total of all amounts reported on line 20 for all properties	23e		
24 **Income.** Add positive amounts shown on line 21. **Do not** include any losses		24	
25 **Losses.** Add royalty losses from line 21 and rental real estate losses from line 22. Enter total losses here .		25	( )
26 **Total rental real estate and royalty income or (loss).** Combine lines 24 and 25. Enter the result here. If Parts II, III, IV, and line 40 on page 2 do not apply to you, also enter this amount on Schedule 1 (Form 1040 or 1040-SR), line 5, or Form 1040-NR, line 18. Otherwise, include this amount in the total on line 41 on page 2		26	

For Paperwork Reduction Act Notice, see the separate instructions.   Cat. No. 11344L   Schedule E (Form 1040 or 1040-SR) 2019

At-Risk Rules

When rental expenditures exceed rental revenue and the rental property is classified a "residence," the amount of rental expenses taxpayers can deduct against rental income is limited by tax regulations.

Two more sets of restrictions may influence the taxpayer's ability to deduct losses originating from rental activities for rental property that is not designated a "residence": the at-risk rules and the passive activity loss rules. These restrictions apply not just to rental operations, but also to losses incurred in any trade, business, or income-producing activity. The at-risk guidelines are covered first, followed by the rules for passive activity loss.

The at-risk rules limit a taxpayer's loss to the amount the taxpayer may genuinely lose (i.e. be out of pocket for) as a result of the action. This is known as the taxpayer's "at-risk" sum. The at-risk regulations apply to any activity conducted as a trade or business (as stated on Schedule C) or for the purpose of earning money (reported on Schedule E). The risk of a taxpayer in any activity equals the following:

1. The monetary value and adjusted basis (cost + improvements accumulated depreciation) of any property contributed to the activity, plus
2. Amounts borrowed for use in the activity if the taxpayer is personally liable for the loan or pledges personal assets as collateral.
3. Any amounts that are not borrowed but are guaranteed payment by the taxpayer, including payment of rents and other amounts that are due from the activity
4. Any amounts of the activity's income that the taxpayer is personally liable for, such as guaranteed payments for services or management fees.

Form 6198, At-Risk Limits, is used by taxpayers who experience a loss from an at-risk activity to calculate their deductible loss. Taxpayers can only deduct losses if they have money at stake. As taxpayers subtract losses from the activity on their tax returns and take withdrawals from the activity, their amount at risk reduces. When the taxpayer's loss is less than the amount at risk in a given year, the taxpayer can deduct the full loss, and the amount at risk is reduced by the amount deducted. This (lower) at-risk amount becomes the taxpayer's at-risk amount at the start of the next year.

> In 20x1, Rasheed starts his own business by contributing $10,000 cash from his personal funds and by getting a $100,000 interest-only loan. Rasheed uses his personal assets to secure the loan. Rasheed's initial amount at-risk is $110,000. During 20x1, the business suffers a $60,000 loss. William can deduct the entire $60,000 loss on his tax return. His amount at-risk is reduced to $50,000.

When the amount of the loss exceeds the taxpayer's amount at risk in a given year, the taxpayer's loss deduction is limited to the amount at risk. Any prohibited loss is carried over to the following year. Because the amount at risk has been lowered to zero, no more losses will be permitted until the taxpayer receives a positive amount at risk. This can be accomplished in a variety of ways. The taxpayer may, for example, make further investments in the business or have the activity take out a debt for which the taxpayer is personally liable.

> Continuing from above, in 20x2, Rasheed's business suffers another $60,000 loss. Since Rasheed's amount at-risk is $50,000, he will only be allowed to deduct $50,000 of his 20x2 losses. He carries over the $10,000 disallowed loss to 20x3.

Losses in Passive Activity

Taxpayers must evaluate the passive activity loss rules after applying the at-risk rules. Losses incurred by passive activities can only be countered by revenue and benefits created by passive activities.

Excess passive losses are carried forward by taxpayers to offset passive income in future tax years. When a taxpayer sells his or her whole investment in a passive activity, any suspended losses that remain are completely deductible in that year.

Definition of Passive Activity Income
The passive activity guidelines divide all revenue and losses into three categories: active, portfolio, and passive. Wages, salaries, and revenue through tangible engagement in a trade or company are examples of active income. Portfolio income is generated by assets that pay out dividends and interest. Gains from the selling of securities (stocks and bonds) are also included in portfolio income. Passive income is typically generated by *(1) a trade or business in which the taxpayer does not engage meaningfully, (2) rental operations, and (3) limited partnerships.*

Either of these three acts may result in a loss. Capital losses result from the selling of portfolio investments. Losses that are not characterized as portfolio losses, on the other hand, are either active or passive. This distinction is significant because taxpayers can deduct losses from active operations from both portfolio and passive income. They can only balance passive activity losses against revenue from other passive activities.

Active income and losses result from material engagement in a trade or business. Material participation happens when the taxpayer is regularly, continuously, and significantly involved in the functioning of the activity. The material involvement criteria can be reached if the taxpayer engages in the activity for more than 500 hours during the year, with the exception of rental real estate operations (which must meet a harsher standard, as mentioned below). (Participation by the owner's spouse is deemed involvement by the owner for the purposes of the 500-hour test.)
Another approach to achieve this criterion is for the taxpayer to participate in the activity for more than 100 hours during the year and to participate at least as much as any other individual, including employees. IRS Publication 925 describes other ways to meet the material participation requirement.

Kevin and Beth jointly own and work for a business that does not involve rental realty. Beth also works part-time as an employee. During the year she works 425 hours for the business, and 600 hours as an employee.

Kevin is not employed elsewhere and spends 40 hours a week working for the business. Because his hours of participation exceed 500, Kevin materially participates in the business. Beth does not participate in the business more than 500 hours, and although her hours exceed 100, her hours do not equal Kevin's hours. Thus, unless she can meet the material participation requirements another way, the passive activity loss rules would apply to Ginny with respect to this activity.

Same facts as above, except that Beth averages 10 hours a week working for the business. Since her 520 hours (10 × 52 weeks) exceed 500, she materially participates in the activity. Thus, the business would not be considered a passive activity.

The majority of rental operations are classified as passive under tax legislation. There are, however, exceptions. One exemption applies to taxpayers engaged in the rental of real estate. Rental activities that: *(1) have an average rental period of less than eight days (e.g., a video rental store); (2) have an average rental period of less than 31 days and provide significant personal services (e.g., motels and hotels); and (3) are incidental to the taxpayer's business are also exempt.*

Losses from rental activities are considered passive losses unless one of the three exceptions occurs.

The Tax Cuts and Jobs Act (TCJA) made some changes to the rules for rental activities. The TCJA added a new provision to the Internal Revenue Code, known as the Qualified Business Income (QBI) deduction, which allows eligible taxpayers to deduct up to 20% of their qualified business income from a qualified trade or business, including rental activities. However, the QBI deduction has some limitations and restrictions based on factors such as the type of trade or business and the taxpayer's taxable income.

Additionally, the CARES Act, passed in 2020, temporarily suspended the limitation on excess business losses for non-corporate taxpayers, including those with rental activities, for tax years

2018 through 2020. This means that taxpayers with rental losses could potentially deduct the full amount of those losses against their other income during those years.

It's also worth noting that the exceptions to the passive loss rules mentioned above still apply under current tax law. However, taxpayers should be aware that the rules for determining whether an activity is considered a rental activity and whether it meets one of the exceptions can be complex, and it's important to carefully review the applicable tax rules and regulations.

Rental Real Estate Losses
Even if one of the seven ways to fulfill the material involvement criteria has been accomplished, rental real estate activities are often classified as passive. Nonetheless, if the taxpayer meets each of the following criteria, a rental real estate operation may qualify as an active trade or business:

1. More than half of the taxpayer's personal services rendered throughout the year are conducted in a real estate trade or business, and
2. The taxpayer performs at least 750 hours of personal service in the real estate trade or company.

If the taxpayer fulfills both conditions, the rental real estate operation is not deemed passive, and any losses from the activity are fully deductible against ordinary income (subject to the already mentioned at-risk restrictions).

A married pair passes the two criteria only if one spouse meets both criterion independently. Couples, in other words, cannot combine their time and energy to achieve the two requirements for rental real estate operations. If these requirements are not satisfied, the rental real estate business is classified as passive.

> Same facts as earlier, except that Kevin and Beth business involves rental realty. Kevin performs more than 750 hours of personal services in businesses involving real property. In addition, this work is more than 50% of his total hours of personal services rendered during the year. Thus, Kevin materially participates in the rental realty business. Beth's hours, on the other hand, do not exceed 750. Thus, Beth is not a material participant in the business. Accordingly, the business is a passive activity to Beth.

> A husband and wife each work 400 hours in a rental realty business. Although as a couple they work more than 750 hours in the rental realty business, the tax laws require that at least one spouse meet the two conditions for material participation. Thus, the rental activity is a passive activity to the couple.

NOTE: *The taxpayer has the burden of providing proof that any personal service tests have been met. To do this, taxpayers should keep a daily log of their hours spent on the activity to prove their hours of participation in the activity.*

Special Deduction of $25,000 for Active Participants

Taxpayers who are not engaged in a "real estate trade or business" and have rental real estate losses may be allowed to deduct up to $25,000 in rental real estate losses from active and portfolio income.

For married taxpayers filing separately who live apart at all times during the year, the deduction maximum is $12,500. Married taxpayers filing separately are not eligible for a special deduction if the pair lived together at any point over the year. To be eligible for this unique deduction, the taxpayer must fulfill both of the following conditions:

1. The taxpayer actively engages in the rental real estate business; and
2. The taxpayer owns at least 10% of the total value of all interests in the activity throughout the course of the year.

Material participation and active participation are two distinct notions. Active participation needs less effort than material participation. Regular, ongoing, and meaningful involvement is not required for active participation. But, it does necessitate extensive and meaningful taxpayer participation in management choices. Approving new tenants, agreeing on rental conditions, authorizing modifications or repairs, or arranging for others to provide services such as repairs are examples of this degree of engagement.

> Going back to the earlier example, although Beth's hours do not constitute material participation, they do indicate active participation in the rental realty business. Since Beth owns at least 10% of the business, she qualifies for the $25,000 special deduction. Thus, in years in which the activity produces a net loss, Beth may be able to deduct up to $25,000 of her share of the loss against her active and portfolio income.

If the taxpayer's adjusted AGI exceeds $100,000 ($50,000 for married taxpayers filing separately), the $25,000 yearly deduction is decreased by 50%. As a result, when modified AGI hits $150,000 ($75,000 for married taxpayers filing separately), the deduction is entirely phased out. Passive losses cannot exceed passive income when calculating adjusted AGI.

Rachel, a single taxpayer, earned $110,000 from her job, $15,000 of passive income from a non–real estate activity, and $20,000 of interest income. Rachel also incurred a $50,000 loss from a rental real estate activity in which she actively participates. Rachel made a $5,500 deductible IRA contribution in 2020. Under the general rule, passive losses usually can offset only passive income. Therefore, Rachel can use $15,000 of her $50,000 rental real estate loss to offset the $15,000 of the income from the non–real estate passive activity.

Because Rachel is actively involved in the rental real estate activities, she may be able to deduct more than $15,000 of her loss. Rachel computes the additional deduction and passive loss carryover as follows.

Wages	$110,000
Interest income	20,000
Passive income	15,000
Passive losses allowed under the general rule	(15,000)
Modified AGI	$130,000
Less AGI threshold for the phase-out	(100,000)
Amount subject to phase-out $	30,000
	× 50%
Amount of deduction lost due to phase-out	$15,000
Excess passive loss from rental real estate ($50,000 − $15,000)	$35,000
Additional passive loss deduction for active participation in rental real estate ($25,000–$15,000 phase-out)	(10,000)
Passive loss carried forward to 2020	$25,000

Modified AGI does not include the $5,500 IRA deduction or the $35,000 of passive losses in excess of passive income. Rachel will deduct a total of $25,000 of passive activity losses ($15,000 under the general rule and $10,000 special deduction) against passive activity income of $15,000.

Suspended Losses

Passive activity losses not deducted in the current tax year carry forward to the next year. Passive losses that are carried forward must be allocated among the various activities that produced the loss. When multiple passive activities exist, taxpayers must determine the suspended loss for each separate activity using the following formula.

Total disallowed loss × (Loss from separate activity/Sum of all losses)

Denny reports the following income and losses from his four passive activities for 20x1.

Activity A	($40,000)
Activity B	30,000
Activity C	(32,000)
Activity D	(8,000)
Net passive loss	($50,000)

Denny allocates his $50,000 net passive loss to activities A, C, and D (the activities producing a total of $80,000 of losses) as follows:

Activity A ($50,000 × $40,000/$80,000)	($25,000)
Activity C ($50,000 × $32,000/$80,000)	(20,000)
Activity D ($50,000 × $8,000/$80,000)	(5,000)
Total suspended losses	($50,000)

These suspended losses carry forward indefinitely as deductions associated with the activity to which each relates. Thus, the $25,000 passive loss carryover associated with Activity A is added to/netted against any passive income (loss) generated by Activity A in 20x2. This net amount becomes Denny's passive income (loss) from Activity A for 20x2. The same process is applied to Activities C and D.

Disposing of A Passive Activity

When taxpayers sell a passive activity, any suspended losses related to that activity are fully deductible. Taxpayers must dispose of their complete stake in the activity in a fully taxed transaction to qualify for this classification. Moreover, the new property owner cannot be a sibling (sister or brother), ancestor (father, grandparent, etc.), or descendant (child, grandchild, etc.) of the taxpayer. When a taxpayer transfers a passive activity through a gift or inheritance, certain regulations apply.

This book does not cover these rules. The income or loss from the selling of a passive activity is treated differently. If a loss occurs, the loss is classified as either ordinary or capital, depending on the circumstances. Because the loss is not considered passive, it is not confined to balancing just passive revenue.

> Continuing with from above, if Denny sells Activity A in 20x2, any part of the $25,000 passive loss carryover from 20x1 that is not utilized in 20x2 to offset passive income and gains is deducted against Denny's active and portfolio income.

Reporting Passive Activity Losses

Passive activity income or loss taxpayers complete Form 8582, Passive Activity Loss Limits, to calculate the amount of passive loss permitted from such activities. The taxpayer then reports the allowable passive loss on the relevant tax form or schedule. Taxpayers, for example, record the passive loss permitted from rental activity on Form E.

Taxpayers file only one Form 8582, regardless of the number or complexity of passive activities. Form 8582 is completed by taxpayers to assess if the passive loss rules prohibit any of the losses reported on the other forms and schedules.

Form 8582 is divided into three sections. Part I requires taxpayers to disclose net income (line 1a), net loss (line 1b), and prior year carry forwards (line 1c) from active rental real estate activities. In addition, they disclose net income (line 3a), net loss (line 3b), and prior year carry forwards (line 3c) from all other passive activities in Part I. The taxpayers' passive income and losses are then combined (line 4). If net income is generated, taxpayers must record the net amount on the applicable tax form or schedule to which the activity pertains (for example, Schedule E for rental real estate).

If there is a net loss, taxpayers go on to Part II to examine if they may use any of the $25,000 special allowance for active engagement in rental real estate operations. Part II requires taxpayers to calculate the amount of net loss available for the $25,000 special allowance. They next calculate their modified adjusted gross income and, if applicable, the amount of phase-out that applies (lines 6–9). Section IV is where taxpayers compute the passive income and loss reported on their tax return for that year. Deductible passive losses (line 16) equal total passive income (lines 1a and 3a) plus Part II special allowance amount (line 10).

Form **8582**	**Passive Activity Loss Limitations** ▶ See separate instructions. ▶ Attach to Form 1040 or Form 1041. ▶ Go to *www.irs.gov/Form8582* for instructions and the latest information.		OMB No. 1545-1008 **2018** Attachment Sequence No. **88**
Department of the Treasury Internal Revenue Service (99)			
Name(s) shown on return		Identifying number	

Part I   **2018 Passive Activity Loss**
Caution: Complete Worksheets 1, 2, and 3 before completing Part I.

Rental Real Estate Activities With Active Participation (For the definition of active participation, see Special Allowance for Rental Real Estate Activities in the instructions.)

1a	Activities with net income (enter the amount from Worksheet 1, column (a))	1a	
b	Activities with net loss (enter the amount from Worksheet 1, column (b))	1b (	)
c	Prior years' unallowed losses (enter the amount from Worksheet 1, column (c))	1c (	)
d	Combine lines 1a, 1b, and 1c	1d	

Commercial Revitalization Deductions From Rental Real Estate Activities

2a	Commercial revitalization deductions from Worksheet 2, column (a)	2a (	)
b	Prior year unallowed commercial revitalization deductions from Worksheet 2, column (b)	2b (	)
c	Add lines 2a and 2b	2c (	)

All Other Passive Activities

3a	Activities with net income (enter the amount from Worksheet 3, column (a))	3a	
b	Activities with net loss (enter the amount from Worksheet 3, column (b))	3b (	)
c	Prior years' unallowed losses (enter the amount from Worksheet 3, column (c))	3c (	)
d	Combine lines 3a, 3b, and 3c	3d	
4	Combine lines 1d, 2c, and 3d. If this line is zero or more, stop here and include this form with your return; all losses are allowed, including any prior year unallowed losses entered on line 1c, 2b, or 3c. Report the losses on the forms and schedules normally used	4	

If line 4 is a loss and: • Line 1d is a loss, go to Part II.
• Line 2c is a loss (and line 1d is zero or more), skip Part II and go to Part III.
• Line 3d is a loss (and lines 1d and 2c are zero or more), skip Parts II and III and go to line 15.

Caution: If your filing status is married filing separately and you lived with your spouse at any time during the year, **do not** complete Part II or Part III. Instead, go to line 15.

Part II   **Special Allowance for Rental Real Estate Activities With Active Participation**
Note: Enter all numbers in Part II as positive amounts. See instructions for an example.

5	Enter the **smaller** of the loss on line 1d or the loss on line 4	5	
6	Enter $150,000. If married filing separately, see instructions . .	6	
7	Enter modified adjusted gross income, but not less than zero (see instructions)	7	

Note: If line 7 is greater than or equal to line 6, skip lines 8 and 9, enter -0- on line 10. Otherwise, go to line 8.

8	Subtract line 7 from line 6	8	
9	Multiply line 8 by 50% (0.50). **Do not** enter more than $25,000. If married filing separately, see instructions	9	
10	Enter the **smaller** of line 5 or line 9	10	

If line 2c is a loss, go to Part III. Otherwise, go to line 15.

Part III   **Special Allowance for Commercial Revitalization Deductions From Rental Real Estate Activities**
Note: Enter all numbers in Part III as positive amounts. See the example for Part II in the instructions.

11	Enter $25,000 reduced by the amount, if any, on line 10. If married filing separately, see instructions	11	
12	Enter the loss from line 4	12	
13	Reduce line 12 by the amount on line 10	13	
14	Enter the **smallest** of line 2c (treated as a positive amount), line 11, or line 13	14	

Part IV   **Total Losses Allowed**

15	Add the income, if any, on lines 1a and 3a and enter the total	15	
16	**Total losses allowed** from all passive activities for 2018. Add lines 10, 14, and 15. See instructions to find out how to report the losses on your tax return	16	

For Paperwork Reduction Act Notice, see instructions.   Cat. No. 63704F   Form **8582** (2018)

Chapter 7

Property: Nontaxable Exchanges and Basis

A gain or loss is frequently realized when taxpayers sell or otherwise dispose of property. This chapter describes how taxpayers calculate their earnings and losses. It also clarifies the profits and losses people are required to record on their tax returns. The chapter starts by explaining the method for calculating realized gains and losses when selling property.

The taxpayer's economic gain or loss from the transaction is reflected in realized profits and losses. These are the difference between the transaction amount and the taxpayer's adjusted basis in the property. A realized gain occurs when the amount realized exceeds the adjusted basis. When the amount realized is less than the adjusted basis, a realized loss occurs. The chapter contains the rules for calculating the amount realized and adjusted basis.

Although selling property generates a realized gain or loss, not all realized profits and losses are declared on the tax return. Taxpayers are generally taxed on all realized gains but can deduct only realized losses resulting from the disposition of investment or commercial property.

Property destroyed through a catastrophe or theft is an exception to this rule. Although the general rule prohibits taxpayers from deducting losses from the sale of personal-use goods, Chapter 5 discussed the rules for the (itemized) deduction for nonbusiness casualty or theft losses. This chapter introduces further exceptions.

Profit or loss realized

When taxpayers sell, swap, or otherwise dispose of property, they realize profits or losses. These also happen when the government utilizes its entitlement to seize taxpayer property in return for just recompense (a process known as condemnation). The difference between the amount realized from the sale and the adjusted basis in the property given up is a realized gain. The difference between the adjusted basis and the amount realized is a realized loss. To put it another way,

Realized gain (loss) = Amount realized − Adjusted basis

Amount Realized

The amount realized is the difference between the sales price and the selling expenses. Selling expenditures include commissions, legal fees, and other transaction-related costs. The sales price is the total of the property's fair market value (FMV) (including cash) plus the services acquired in exchange for the property given up. It also includes any debt owed by the taxpayer (seller) that is assumed by the buyer. (When the buyer takes the seller's obligation, it is analogous to the buyer giving the seller cash to pay off the loan.

> Robin sells stock for $12,000 cash plus a car valued at $5,000. Robin's amount realized is $17,000 ($12,000 + $5,000).

> Maria exchanges land for a building that has a FMV of $90,000. The land is subject to a $50,000 mortgage, which the other party assumes. Maria's amount realized is $140,000 ($90,000 + $50,000).

Adjusted Basis

When disposing of property, the tax laws allow taxpayers to recover their investment in property tax free. Basis is the term used to describe the taxpayer's investment in property. Taxpayers realize a gain when the amount realized exceeds their basis in the property.

If the entire basis is not recovered, taxpayers realize a loss for the unrecovered amount. Between the time taxpayers acquire property and the time they dispose of it, events may occur that require taxpayers to adjust their basis in property. Adjusted basis is the term for the taxpayer's investment in property after making those adjustments. Adjusted basis can be stated as follows:

Adjusted basis = Initial basis in property + Capital additions − Capital recoveries.

The initial basis of purchased property usually is its cost. However, taxpayers can acquire property in other ways, such as through gift or inheritance. The initial basis of a property depends on how the taxpayer acquired it.

Capital Additions
Capital additions include the expenditures of transferring or defending property title. Commissions and legal fees are two examples of such expenses. Capital additions also include the expense of renovations that raise the value of the property, extend its useful life, or convert it to a new use. Improvements have a useful life of more than a year. Maintenance and repairs are not considered upgrades because they are recurrent expenditures.

Examples of Improvements
◆ *Installing a new furnace or roof*
◆ *Putting up a fence*
◆ *Paving a driveway*
◆ *Rebuilding a car engine*
◆ *Landscaping*
◆ *Building a recreation room in an unfinished basement*
◆ *Paying special assessments for sidewalks, roads, etc.*
◆ *Adding a room onto a house or other building*

Years ago, Leroy paid $125,000 for a house that he uses as a vacation home. Over the years, Leroy has paid $35,000 to remodel the kitchen, $5,000 to install a wooden fence around the property, and $3,000 to reshingle the roof. He also has paid $13,800 to keep the property in good condition. Leroy's adjusted basis in the home is $168,000 ($125,000 + $35,000 + $5,000 + $3,000). Since the vacation home is a personal belonging, the $13,800 spent on repairs and maintenance are nondeductible personal expenses. If Leroy were to sell the home, his realized gain or loss would be the difference between the amount realized from the sale and his $168,000 adjusted basis in the home.

Capital Recoveries

Capital recoveries are a return on the taxpayer's property investment. These occur when taxpayers get money or claim tax breaks related to the property. When taxpayers recoup a portion of their investment in property before disposing of it, their basis in the property must be reduced proportionally.

When property is damaged in a casualty, taxpayers deduct the amount received from the insurance company from their basis in the property. The same base reduction criterion applies to monies received by taxpayers from the government in exchange for the government's use of a portion of their property (known as an easement). The sums received by taxpayers from the insurance company or the government constitute a return on their initial investment in the property. The taxpayer has less invested in the property after receiving these monies. As a result, the taxpayer's basis (investment) in the property must be lowered.

> Several years ago, Sheldon paid $120,000 for land. In the current year, He receives $20,000 from the government in exchange for the right to use part of the land. Sheldon must reduce his basis in the land by $20,000. Although he initially paid $120,000 for the land, after receiving $20,000 from the government, his net investment in the land is $100,000. Ralph's adjusted basis in the land equals $100,000 ($120,000 initial basis − $20,000 capital recovery).

Taxpayers also lower their basis in property by deducting amounts related to the property on their tax filings. This includes sums reduced for loss due to a casualty or theft. It also includes depreciation deductions, such as bonus depreciation and Section 179 expenditure.

Xhosa is a sole proprietor. During the year, Xhosa placed in service equipment costing $24,000. She elected to expense the entire amount under Section 179. Xhosa's adjusted basis in the equipment is $0. Thus, the entire amount realized on the sale of the equipment will result in realized gain.

In 1993, Lee paid $62,000 for a building. Lee spent $10,000 in 1999 for a new roof. In 2006, a fire damaged the building. The insurance company paid Lee $20,000 for the loss. Lee claimed a $10,000 casualty loss deduction on her 2006 tax return for the unreimbursed portion of the loss. In 2007, Lee spent $29,000 to rebuild the part of the building destroyed in the fire. Over the years, Lee has deducted $22,000 for depreciation on the building. Lee computes the adjusted basis in the building as follows.

Initial basis in the building		$62,000
Capital additions Improvements	$10,000	
Restoration costs	29,000	39,000
Minus capital recoveries		
Depreciation deductions	$22,000	
Insurance proceeds	20,000	
Casualty loss deduction	10,000	(52,000)
Adjusted basis in the building		$49,000

Initial Basis

Taxpayers begin with the initial basis when calculating their adjusted basis in property. The cost of the bought property serves as the first basis. Taxpayers can, however, acquire property via other ways, such as gifts, inheritances, and divorce settlements.

Property Bought by Purchase

The cost of the bought property serves as the first basis (what the taxpayer gives up to buy the property). It includes money borrowed by taxpayers to purchase the property. It also covers any fees spent to secure clear title to the property or to make it fit for usage. These are some examples of such expenses:

Purchased with sales or excise taxes
Survey and title insurance fees
Costs incurred in delivering, installing, and testing the property
Fees for recording, legal counsel, and accounting

> Wade buys real estate, paying $50,000 cash and assuming the seller's $75,000 mortgage on the property. Wade's initial basis is $125,000 ($50,000 + $75,000).

When a taxpayer exchanges services for property, the taxpayer's initial basis in the property is the value of the services included in income.

> Sal received ten shares of stock in exchange for services he rendered. The market value of the shares is $300. Sal is taxed on $300 for his services. His initial basis in the shares is $300.

Purchasing at a Discount

Companies will occasionally sell items or other property to their employees for less than FMV. Employees are frequently taxed on the difference between the FMV and the purchase price. Because the first basis includes monies taxed as income, the employee's initial basis equals the FMV of the property in these circumstances. If the employee is not required to declare any income from the bargain purchase (as with a qualified employee discount), the employee's initial basis is equal to the amount paid for the property.

> Adam pays $60 for property from a company where he is an employee. The FMV of the property is $100. Adam reports the $40 difference between FMV and the purchase price on his tax return. Adam's initial basis in the property equals $100 ($60 purchase price + $40 reported in income).

Basket Purchases

A single purchasing amount can sometimes acquire more than one home. Different depreciation rules might apply to various properties. Also, taxpayers may sell the homes at different points in the future. For these reasons, the purchase money must be divided among the purchased properties. Taxpayers divide the purchase payment among the properties based on their respective FMVs. The amount allotted to a single property equals the acquisition price multiplied by the property's FMV to the total FMV of all properties.

Initial basis = Purchase price × (FMV of the property/FMV of all properties)

> Deontay pays $90,000 for land and a building. At the time of the purchase, the FMV of the land and building are $80,000 and $40,000, respectively. Deontay's basis in the land equals $60,000 [$90,000 × ($80,000/$120,000)]. His basis in the building equals $30,000 [$90,000 × ($40,000/$120,000)].

Property Received From A Spouse

When a taxpayer gets property from a spouse, the taxpayer inherits the spouse's adjusted basis in the property. When property is transferred between spouses, there are no tax ramifications (or former spouses when the transfer is part of a divorce settlement).

> As part of a divorce settlement, Drew transferred to April title to his mountain cabin. Drew paid $80,000 for the cabin six years prior to his marriage to April. Over the years, he spent $23,500 on improvements to the cabin. At the time of the transfer, the cabin was worth $240,000. April's basis in the home equals Drew's adjusted basis in the home $103,500 ($80,000 + $23,500). If April were to sell the home for its current fair market value, her realized gain would be $136,500 ($240,000 − $103,500).

Inherited Property

When someone passes away, an executor is appointed to distribute the decedent's possessions (known as the estate). The executor must first calculate the estate tax payable before distributing the inheritance to the decedent's heirs. The estate tax is calculated based on the entire FMV of the decedent's estate (net of liabilities). Inheritance tax is only levied when the value of the estate surpasses a specified threshold.

The executor normally values the estate on the date of the decedent's death for calculating the estate tax

(DOD). The starting basis of an heir in an inherited property is the property's FMV on the DOD. In certain circumstances, the executor may choose to value the estate six months later (known as the alternative valuation date, or AVD). When the executor values the estate on the AVD, the heir's initial basis in the inherited property is the FMV on the AVD or the day the property is delivered to the heir, whichever comes first.

> Rhonda inherited land from her grandfather, who died on November 5, 2013. On that day, the land was valued at $45,000. On May 5, 2014, its value was $42,000. The land was distributed to Rhonda on July 2, 2014. Rhonda's basis in the land is $45,000 if DOD is used to value the grandfather's estate. If the AVD is used, Rhonda's basis is $42,000 (since the AVD occurs before the date of distribution).

> Same facts as above, except that the land was distributed to Rhonda on March 10, 2014, when its value was $43,000. If DOD is used to value the grandfather's estate, Rhonda's basis in the land is still $45,000. If the AVD is used, Rhonda's basis is $43,000 (since the distribution date occurs first).

The Tax Relief, Unemployment Insurance Reauthorization, and Job Creation Act of 2010 reinstated the estate tax for individuals who died in 2010 and provided a modified carryover basis system for valuing assets for estate tax purposes. The American Taxpayer Relief Act of 2012 made this reinstatement permanent and set the estate tax exemption amount at $5 million, indexed for inflation. In 2023, the estate tax exemption amount is $12.06 million. Therefore, taxpayers who inherit property from decedents after 2010 should refer to current IRS publications and regulations for guidance on how to determine the basis of inherited property.

Gifted Property

Property obtained as a gift is subject to two sets of restrictions. One set of rules applies where the FMV of the property at the time of the donation is less than the donor's adjusted basis in the property. When the FMV exceeds the donor's adjusted basis in the property, another set of rules applies.

FMV is less than the donor's basis.
When the FMV of the property is less than the donor's (adjusted) basis at the time of the gift, the donee's basis in the property remains unknown until the donee (the person receiving the gift) disposes of the property. When disposing, the donee first computes gain or loss using the FMV.

The donee's initial basis is the value of the property at the time of the gift. If a loss occurs, the donee's initial basis is the fair market value at the time of the gift. If there is a gain, the donor's basis is normally the donee's original basis. If the second computation yields no gain, there is no gain or loss, and the donee's adjusted basis equals the amount realized.

> Selena receives stock valued at $15,000 as a gift. The donor paid $20,000 for the stock. Selena later sells the stock for $23,000. Since Joan sells the stock for more than the donor's basis, her basis in the stock is $20,000. Joan realizes a $3,000 gain ($23,000 amount realized − $20,000 basis).

> Same facts as in example above, except that Selena
> sells the stock for $13,000. Selena sells the stock for
> less than the $15,000 FMV. Thus, her basis in the stock
> is $15,000, and she realizes a $2,000 loss ($13,000
> amount realized − $15.000 basis).

> Same facts as above, except that Selena sells the stock
> for $17,000. When Selena uses the $15,000 FMV
> ("loss basis") to compute her loss, a $2,000 gain
> results. When she uses the donor's $20,000 adjusted
> basis ("gain basis"), a $3,000 loss results. Thus, Selena
> realizes neither a gain nor a loss. Her basis in the stock
> equals $17,000 (the amount realized from the sale).

When the gifted property is depreciable property to
the donee, the donee uses the donor's basis to
compute depreciation expense.

The FMV exceeds the Donor's Basis

If the FMV of the property at the time of the
donation exceeds the donor's basis, the donee takes
over the donor's basis. If the donor paid gift tax on
the transfer, the donee deducts the gift tax from the
basis. For gifts given prior to 1977, the donee's
basis is increased by the amount of the gift tax.
After 1976, just a portion of the gift tax is applied to
the donee's basis. This percentage is equal to the
ratio of the rise in value of the property while
owned by the donor (FMV at the time of the gift
giver's basis) to the taxable value of the donation. In
all circumstances, the donee's basis cannot be
greater than the fair market value of the property at
the time of the gift.

Same facts as above, except that the gift occurred in 1973. Millie still takes her uncle's basis in the property, but adds 100% of the gift tax to arrive at her initial basis in the property. Millie's initial basis would be $45,000 ($30,000 + $15,000), as this amount is less than the $75,000 FMV of the gifted property.

In 1993 Millie received property from her uncle worth $75,000. The uncle paid $15,000 in gift tax on the transfer. The uncle's adjusted basis in the property was $30,000. Since the FMV exceeds the uncle's basis, Millie takes her uncle's $30,000 basis. While her uncle owned the property, it went up in value by $45,000 ($75,000 − $30,000). If the taxable value of the gift is $75,000, Millie adds 60% ($45,000 ÷ $75,000) of the gift tax to her basis. Millie's initial basis in the gifted property would be $39,000 [$30,000 + (60% × $15,000)].

Property Converted to Business or Rental Use

Taxpayers can convert their personal items to use in a company or rental activity instead of purchasing new property. Taxpayers, for example, can transform their residences into rental property or begin utilizing their own automobiles or computers in their enterprises. The basis of converted property, like gifted property, is governed by two sets of regulations. The first set of rules applies if the property's FMV at the time of conversion is more than the taxpayer's adjusted basis in the property. If the FMV is less than the taxpayer's adjusted basis, a different set of rules applies.

The FMV exceeds the Adjusted Basis (Appreciated Property)

When taxpayers convert appreciated property, the general rule is used to calculate the adjusted basis:

Capital additions + initial basis = capital recoveries.

If the converted property is depreciable, they compute depreciation expenditure using the amended basis at the time of conversion.

On May 4, 20x6, Selena converted her home into rental property. Selena paid $93,630 for the home in 20x0. Over the years she has made improvements to the home totaling $25,300. Thus, her adjusted basis in the home is $118,930 ($93,630 + $25,300). On May 4, 20x6, the home is worth $155,300. Selena's adjusted basis in the rental property is $118,930, since the FMV at the time of the conversion exceeds that amount. Donna uses this amount (minus the cost of the land) to compute her depreciation expense in 20x6.

FMV is less than the adjusted basis.

When taxpayers convert depreciated property, the adjusted basis of the property is computed at the time of disposal. Taxpayers utilize the usual rule for calculating adjusted basis to determine realized gains:

Starting base + all capital additions + all capital recoveries.

They apply the formula:
FMV at conversion + postconversion capital additions + postconversion capital recoveries
to calculate realized losses.

If the converted property is depreciable, taxpayers compute depreciation expenditure using the FMV of the property at the time of conversion.

On January 1, 20x0, Emily converted her home to rental property. At the time of the conversion, the FMV of the home was $50,000. Emily paid $56,000 for the home and made $4,000 of capital improvements prior to 20x0. After converting the property, Emily deducted $6,000 for depreciation and made $3,000 in capital improvements. Emily sells the property for $59,000. Since at the time of conversion the $50,000 FMV was less than $60,000 the adjusted basis ($56,000 + $4,000 preconversion improvements), Emily computes an adjusted basis for gain and an adjusted basis for loss. Emily also uses the $50,000 FMV, minus the FMV of the land, as her basis for depreciating the home.

Initial basis	$56,000
Plus all capital additions	
($4,000 + $3,000)	7,000
Minus all capital recoveries	(6,000)
Adjusted basis for gain	$57,000
FMV at conversion	$50,000
Plus postconversion capital additions	3,000
Minus postconversion capital recoveries	(6,000)
Adjusted basis for loss	$47,000

Because the amount realized exceeds the adjusted basis for gain, Emily sells the property for a gain. Using an adjusted basis of $57,000, Emily realizes a $2,000 gain ($59,000 − $57,000). Had Emily sold the property for a loss (an amount realized less than $47,000), her adjusted basis would have been $47,000. Had the amount realized been between $47,000 and $57,000, Emily would have realized no gain or loss, and her adjusted basis would be the amount realized.

Adjusted Basis in Converted Property

When at conversion FMV > adjusted basis,
Adjusted basis = Initial basis + all capital additions
− all capital recoveries
Depreciable basis = Adjusted basis (minus the cost
of the land, if any)

When at conversion FMV < adjusted basis,
Adjusted basis for gains = Initial basis + all capital
additions − all capital recoveries
Adjusted basis for losses = FMV at conversion +
postconversion capital additions − postconversion
capital recoveries
Depreciable basis = FMV at conversion (minus the
FMV of the land, if any)

Special Rules for Stock Ownership

When taxpayers purchase stock, their basis equals the purchase price plus any commissions or transfer fees paid. If taxpayers acquire stock through other sources (gift, inheritance, etc.), the procedures for calculating adjusted basis provided previously in the chapter apply.

Shares Identification

Taxpayers can buy identical shares of stock in the same firm for different amounts at different dates. When taxpayers sell stock in that firm, they must specify which shares they are selling. The Internal Revenue Code (Code) mandates taxpayers to employ the first-in, first-out technique if no identification is provided.

In 20x0 Jackson paid $10,000 for 1,000 shares of common stock in ABC corporation. In 20x2 he paid $12,500 for another 1,000 shares. During the current year, Jackson sells 1,000 of his shares in ABC for $11,000. If he does not specify which 1,000 were sold, the tax laws require him to use the $10,000 basis in the earliest shares he purchased. This would result in a $1,000 realized gain ($11,000 amount realized − $10,000 adjusted basis). However, if at the time of the sale, Jackson were to tell his stockbroker that he wanted to sell the 1,000 shares that he purchased in 20x2, he would have a realized loss of $1,500 ($11,000 − $12,500).

Note: *To identify shares sold, taxpayers should deliver the stock certificates to the broker or agent. If a broker or agent holds the stock certificates, then taxpayers should instruct the broker in writing which shares they wish to sell. Taxpayers should request confirmation from the broker as proof that the instructions were followed.*

Stock Splits

Taxpayers who hold stock may subsequently purchase more shares through a stock split or a stock dividend. A stock split occurs when a firm distributes a ratable fraction of extra shares to its stockholders. As a consequence, each shareholder receives extra shares without altering their percentage ownership in the firm. There is no money generated from a stock split. Taxes just apply their adjusted basis in the original shares to any shares held following the split.

Years ago, Angie paid $14,000 for 1,000 shares of stock in ABCO ($14 a share). During the current year, ABCO declared a two-for-one stock split. Each shareholder received two shares of stock for every one share they returned to ABCO. The shareholders of ABCO are not taxed on the split. After the split, Angie owns 2,000 shares of ABCO stock. Her adjusted basis in those shares is her original $14,000 adjusted basis in the stock. Thus, Angie's basis in each share of stock has been reduced to $7 ($14,000/2,000 shares).

Dividends on Stocks

A stock dividend is paid to shareholders when a business pays them a dividend in the form of shares of stock in the firm rather than cash. If shareholders have the option of receiving either a stock or a cash dividend, the cash or FMV of the shares (whichever they select) must be reported on their tax return. If they elect to receive a stock dividend, the stock's FMV becomes their basis in the newly acquired shares.

A nontaxable event occurs when a firm distributes a stock dividend to shareholders without providing them the option of receiving a cash dividend. Taxpayers must assign some basis from the original shares to the shares obtained in the nontaxable stock dividend, just as they do with stock splits. When the stock dividend is of the same class as the original basis, the taxpayer divides the original basis by the entire number of shares. A common stock shareholder getting a common stock dividend is an example of a same class of stock dividend. When the stock dividend is not of the same class as the original shares, the taxpayer allocates the basis in the original shares based on the total shares' relative FMV.

The same formula is used by taxpayers to apportion the purchase price across properties bought in a basket acquisition. A common stock shareholder receiving a preferred stock dividend is an example of a stock payout of a different class.

> Howard paid $1,100 for 50 shares of common stock. This year Howard received five shares of common stock as a nontaxable stock dividend. Howard's basis in 55 shares of common stock is $1,100, or $20 a share.

Return of Capital

Dividends are paid by corporations from their revenues and profits (E&P). In the company balance sheet, E&P is basically equivalent to retained earnings. When a business with no E&P distributes property (including cash) to its shareholders, the distribution is viewed as a return on investment for the shareholder. The amount distributed is not taxable, but the shareholder decreases the basis in the shares by the amount received, as with other capital recoveries. If the amount distributed exceeds the shareholder's basis in the shares, the extra amount is a gain for the shareholder.

Profits and Losses Recognized

Recognized profits and losses are realized gains and losses reported on tax returns by taxpayers. Taxable gains and losses may not come from all realized profits and losses. Taxpayers generally recognize all realized profits but only losses on the sale of company or investment property. In previous chapters, we discussed an exemption to this rule that permits taxpayers to deduct casualty or theft losses on personal-use property. This chapter discusses six additional exceptions to the basic norm.

◆ *Losses involving wash sales*
◆ *Losses from sales between related parties*
◆ *Gains from the sale of qualified small business stock*
◆ *Gains and losses from like-kind exchanges*
◆ *Most gains from the sale of a principal residence Certain gains from involuntary conversions*

Wash Sales

Because securities (stocks and bonds) represent an investment, any realized loss on the sale of securities is normally recognized by the taxpayer. Nevertheless, no loss is permitted if the taxpayer repurchases "substantially similar" stocks within 30 days of the transaction. Wash sales are the word used to characterize these sales and repurchases.

Substantially identical securities are those that are issued by the same corporation and have comparable characteristics. In the case of stocks, essentially identical would be the same stock class with the same voting rights. Bonds with similar interest rates and maturity dates would be considered essentially equal. If the taxpayer merely repurchases a portion of the shares during the 61-day period following the sale, just that portion of the loss is disallowed.

On January 5, 2014, Mike sold 1,000 shares of common stock in Arnold Co. for $5,000. Mike's purchases of Arnold's common stock are shown below.

1,000 shares on June 6, 2011	$8,000
600 shares on November 6, 2013	4,500
250 shares on December 17, 2013	2,000
350 shares on January 10, 2014	3,000

Assuming Tom does not identify which shares were sold, he is assumed to have sold the 1,000 shares purchased on June 6, 2011. The sale results in a $3,000 realized loss ($5,000 − $8,000), which normally would be recognized for tax purposes.

However, since Tom repurchased 600 (250 + 350) of the 1,000 shares between December 6, 2013, and February 4, 2014 (61 days surrounding January 5, 2014), 60% (600 ÷ 1,000) of the loss is disallowed ($3,000 × 60% = $1,800). Tom recognizes a $1,200 loss ($3,000 − $1,800) on the 400 shares sold and not repurchased.

Any loss prohibited as a result of a wash sale is just postponed and will be permitted when the taxpayer sells the (repurchased) shares later. To defer the loss, the taxpayer adds the disallowed loss to the repurchased shares' basis.

Sales between related parties
Taxpayers can normally realize a loss when they sell an investment or commercial property for less than its adjusted basis. Taxpayers, on the other hand, cannot recognize losses when they sell property to a connected party. Individuals and their family members are considered related parties for tax reasons. Spouses, siblings (brothers and sisters), descendants (children, grandkids, etc.), and

ancestors are examples of family members (parents, grandparents, etc.). The disallowed loss, unlike wash sales, does not raise the (connected) buyer's basis in the property. Instead, when the property is eventually sold, the buyer can utilize the disallowed loss to offset any realized gain. The buyer is not permitted to utilize the disallowed loss to generate or enlarge a loss.

> Kay sold stock to his son, Dave, for $10,000. Kay bought the stock several years ago for $16,000. Although stock is investment property, Kay cannot recognize the $6,000 realized loss ($10,000 − $16,000) since he sold the stock to a related party. Dave's basis in the stock is $10,000, the amount he paid for it. If Dave later sells the stock for $12,000, Dave's realized gain is $2,000 ($12,000 − $10,000). Dave can use $2,000 of Kay's disallowed loss to offset this gain. Thus, Dave's recognized gain is $0. Since the disallowed loss can only reduce realized gains and cannot create a loss, the rest of Kay's disallowed loss will never be used.

> Same facts as above, except that Dave sells the stock for $9,000. Dave realizes a $1,000 loss ($9,000 − $10,000). Since a disallowed loss cannot create or increase a loss, Dave cannot use any of Kay's disallowed loss. Dave recognizes the $1,000 loss from the sale, and Kay's entire $6,000 disallowed loss is gone.

Related parties, in addition to persons and their family members, include individuals and companies when an individual holds more than 50% of the voting shares in the corporation. Family members' stock counts as stock held by the person. This type of indirect stock ownership is known as constructive ownership.

Ollie owns 30% of Sky Corporation. The following people own the rest of the stock:
Ollie's aunt 35%
Ollie's brother 25%
Ollie's father 10%

Ollie owns 30% of Sky outright. He constructively owns the 25% owned by his brother and the 10% owned by his father. Ollie's actual plus constructive ownership exceeds 50%.

In a current year, Ollie sells land held as an investment to Sky Corporation for its current FMV of $75,000. Ollie paid $112,000 for the land. Since Ollie's actual and constructive ownership in Sky exceeds 50%, he cannot deduct the $37,000 loss he realizes on the sale ($75,000 amount realized − $112,000 basis). Alpha's basis in the land is the $75,000 it paid for the land.

In a future tax year Sky sells the land for $122,000. Its realized gain is $47,000 ($122,000 − $75,000). Sky can use Ollie's $37,000 disallowed loss to reduce its recognized gain to $10,000.

Qualified Small Business Stock

People can deduct a part of the gain on the sale of Section 1202 eligible small company shares if they hold it for more than five years. The shares must have been bought after August 10, 1993 as part of the corporation's initial issue of stock to qualify for the exclusion. Just a few corporations may issue eligible small company shares. These constraints are outside the scope of this discussion.

Like-Kind Exchanges

Rather of selling property for cash, taxpayers might swap it for other property. When this happens, the difference between the FMV of the property received and the adjusted basis of the property given up results in a realized gain or loss. Taxpayers generally recognize all gains from such transfers but only losses from trades involving company or investment property.

When a trade involves like-kind property, the general rule is broken. Taxpayers do not recognize earnings or losses in a like-kind trade. Instead, realized profits and losses are carried forward. Taxpayers alter the basis of the like-kind property they receive in the exchange to postpone profits and losses until the item is disposed of in a non-like-kind exchange. This new base is also utilized to calculate depreciation on depreciable property.

Basis of the new property = FMV of the new property + Postponed loss − Postponed gain

> Denise exchanges property with an adjusted basis of $100,000 for like-kind property valued at $60,000. Denise realizes a $40,000 loss ($60,000 − $100,000) but does not recognize any of the loss. Denise's basis in the new property equals $100,000 ($60,000 FMV of new property + $40,000 postponed loss). If the new property is depreciable property, she computes depreciation expense using her $100,000 basis in the property.

Like-Kind Property
The rules above outlined apply exclusively to like-kind property transfers. Four elements must be

completed in order for property to qualify as like kind.

1. A straight transaction must take place. Some three-party exchanges may qualify as direct exchanges. A direct exchange can also take place if the property to be received is identified within 45 days of the taxpayer transferring the property and received within 180 days of the taxpayer transferring the property.
2. Both the exchanged and acquired property must be commercial or investment property.
3. Real estate must be traded for other real estate. Personal property (non-real estate tangible property) must be exchanged for equivalent personal property.
4. Inventory, foreign real estate, securities (stocks and bonds), or partnership interests cannot be exchanged.

The like-kind rules must be followed. When all four requirements are satisfied, taxpayers are required to defer any realized gain or loss from the like-kind trade. As a result, to deduct a loss coming from a like-kind exchange, the taxpayer needs to not meet one or more of the four requirements. For example, the taxpayer could fail to meet the requirements for a direct exchange.

Like-Kind Exchanges of Business or Investment Personal Property

To qualify as a like-kind trade, the taxpayer must swap personal property held for business or investment for similarly held personal property. Personal property that is almost identical is referred to be similar. In addition to trades involving comparable functional personal property, the following are examples of virtually identical properties (i.e., like-kind property).

◆ *All office furniture, fixtures, and office equipment (copiers, fax machines, etc.) are like-kind, as are all autos.*

◆ *Computers, printers, and auxiliary equipment are examples of similar items.*

◆ *All light general-purpose vehicles are like-kind property (but light general-purpose trucks and heavy general-purpose trucks are not).*

> A corporation exchanges an automobile for a light general purpose truck. Although both assets are vehicles, they are not considered to be nearly identical. Thus, the like-kind exchange rules would not apply to this exchange. The corporation would recognize gain or loss for the difference between the FMV of the property it receives and the adjusted basis of the property it gives up in the exchange.

> A sole proprietor exchanges a computer for a new printer. The like-kind exchange rules apply to this exchange, as computers, printers, and peripheral equipment (devices that plug into a computer) are all considered to be nearly identical personal property (and therefore, like-kind).

Like-Kind Exchanges of Business or Investment Real Property

For real estate trades, the like-kind exchange rules are more liberal. Real property used for business or investment must be traded for any other real property used for business or investment to qualify as a likekind transaction. Unimproved land kept for investment, for example, might be swapped for a warehouse utilized in the taxpayer's company.

Similarly, an office building utilized in the taxpayer's business can be exchanged for an apartment building maintained for investment purposes.

> A person trades his vacation house for land that he intends to hold as an investment. This exchange is exempt from the like-kind exchange requirements. Although both of the properties transferred are real estate, the vacation house is a personal possession. Real property held for business or investment must be traded for other real property held for business or investment for the like-kind exchange rules to apply.

Boot

Not all like-kind transfers include equal-value properties. When trading unequally valued properties, the person receiving the less valuable property will need more property from the other side. Boot is the non-like-kind property put in to balance out the sale. Boot is frequently associated with currency, although it can also entail other property. Boot happens when one party assumes the debt of the other. The person who adopts (takes up) the debt is considered to be providing boot. The party who is debt-free is said to be receiving boot. Only the net (extra) responsibility counts as boot when both parties assume each other's debt. The amount of gain or loss recorded on like-kind exchanges of boot is determined by whether the taxpayer gave or received boot.

> Sharon exchanges land valued at $100,000 for Tyler's building valued at $80,000. Both properties qualify as like-kind. To even up the deal, Tylerl agrees to assume Sharon's $20,000 liability on the land. Sharon's release from debt is similar to her receiving $20,000 cash and using it to pay off the debt. Thus, Sharon receives $20,000 boot;Tylerl gives $20,000 boot.

In a different scenario, Tyler exchanges land valued at $80,000 for Sharon's building valued at $100,000. Both properties qualify as like-kind. Tyler owes $40,000 on the land; Sharon owes $60,000 on the building. Both parties agree to assume each other's debt. In this exchange, each party receives property worth $140,000. Tyler receives a building worth $100,000 and is relieved of $40,000 of debt. Sharon receives land valued at $80,000 and is relieved of $60,000 of debt. Because the parties assume each other's debt, only the net liability of $20,000 ($60,000 − $40,000) is treated as boot. Tyler takes on more debt than he is relieved of; therefore, Tyler gives $20,000 of boot. Sharon is relieved of more debt than she assumed; therefore, Sharon receives $20,000 of boot.

Recieving Boot

The receipt of boot has no influence on the realized losses from the like-kind exchange. These losses are deferred, increasing the taxpayer's basis in the like-kind property received. Yet, the taxpayer's realized gains are only recognized to the amount of the boot's FMV.

Ken exchanges a machine with an adjusted basis of $47,000 for a machine valued at $45,000 and $5,000 cash. Ken's realized gain equals $3,000 ($50,000 amount realized − $47,000 adjusted basis). Ken receives boot of $5,000; therefore, he recognizes the entire $3,000 gain. Ken's basis in the new machine is its FMV of $45,000 since there is no postponed gain.

Same facts as above, except that Ken's adjusted basis in the old machine is $42,000. Ken realizes an $8,000 gain ($50,000 − $42,000). He recognizes the gain to the extent of the boot received. Therefore, Ken reports a $5,000 gain on his tax return and postpones the rest. Ken reduces the basis in the new machine by the postponed gain ($45,000 FMV − $3,000 postponed gain = $42,000).

Giving Boot

No gain or loss is recorded for the taxpayer who donates boot in a like-kind exchange as long as the FMV of the boot equals the taxpayer's basis in the boot supplied. This occurs when the taxpayer contributes cash or absorbs the debt of the other party. Where the FMV of the boot differs from the taxpayer's basis in the boot delivered, the taxpayer is considered as having sold the boot to the other party and realizes a gain or loss for the difference between the FMV and the taxpayer's basis in the boot. Under the general rule, the taxpayer will recognize gain to the extent that the FMV of the boot exceeds its basis. However, if the FMV is less than the taxpayer's basis in the boot, the taxpayer will recognize a loss only if the boot was business or investment property.

Like-Kind Exchanges Between Related Parties

The like-kind trade rules can be used by related parties. Nonetheless, any postponed gain or loss must be recorded in the disposal year if either (related) party disposes of the like-kind property within two years of the exchange. The basis of the like-kind property is raised or decreased by the realized gain or loss.

> On October 4, 20x1, Sky Enterprises exchanged one parcel of land for another parcel of land with Xavier, Sky's Enterprises's sole shareholder. The land that Xavier exchanged was worth $200,000, and his basis in the land was $150,000. The land that Sky Enterprises exchanged was worth $190,000, and its basis in the land was $190,000. To even up the deal, the company paid Xavier $10,000 cash.

As a result of the like-kind exchange, Xavier realized a $50,000 gain ($200,000 FMV of the properties received − $150,000 basis in the land). He recognized a $10,000 gain (equal to the boot received), and postponed $40,000. Xavier's basis in his new land is $150,000 ($190,000 FMV of the new land − $40,000 postponed gain).

Sky Enterprises, on the other hand, realized no gain or loss on the exchange ($200,000 FMV of the property received − $190,000 adjusted basis in the land − $10,000 cash paid). Its basis in the land received is its $200,000 FMV. On August 5, 20x3, Sky Enterprises sells its new land in a non-like-kind exchange. Because the sale occurs within two years, Xavier must recognize the $40,000 of postponed gain on his 20x3 tax return. Xavier's basis in the land he received in the exchange increases to $190,000 ($150,000 + $40,000 recognized gain).

Selling of a Primary Residence

Personal-use property is the taxpayer's principal abode (main home). As a result, when taxpayers sell their primary residence, they normally register a gain but do not recognize a loss. The Code, however, enables taxpayers to exclude up to $250,000 of the gain. Married couples filing a combined tax return may deduct up to $500,000. To be eligible for the exclusion, taxpayers must have lived in the residence for two of the preceding five years.

Taxpayers who fail to achieve this condition due to a change in job location, the taxpayer's health, or other specified unanticipated causes are eligible for partial exclusions.

To be eligible for the entire exclusion amount, homeowners must own and live in the house as their primary residence for at least two years out of the five years before the date of sale. If the home is used other than as a primary residence after 2008 (for example, rented out or used as a second home), the exclusion amount of $250,000/$500,000 must be reduced by the full exclusion amount multiplied by the ratio: period of nonqualifying use / period of ownership in the previous 5 years.

Consider an unmarried homeowner who has owned a home for 12 years, with five months of nonqualifying usage in the previous five years. The exclusion for the homeowner would be lowered by $20,833 ($250,000 5/60 months). As a result, the homeowner may deduct up to $229,167 ($250,000 - $20,833) of the gain on the sale.

NOTE; *Due to the sizable exclusion ($250,000/$500,000), many taxpayers will not report gain when selling their main home. However, taxpayers still want to keep track of their basis in their home to show that the gain from the sale does not exceed the exclusion amount. This involves keeping a copy of the closing statement and receipts for all capital improvements made to the home. Any taxable gain from the sale is considered investment income for purposes of the 3.8% net investment income.*

> On September 3, 2014, the Duncans sell their main home of 20 years for $200,000. Selling expenses are $10,000. The Duncans paid $50,000 for the home. The Duncans do not recognize any of the $140,000 ($200,000 − $10,000 − $50,000) gain, since this amount is less than $500.000.

Involuntary Conversions

Taxpayers receive a gain or loss on property converted involuntarily. Casualties, thefts, and condemnations are the most prevalent involuntary conversions.

Gains and Losses in Condemnation

When the government uses its power to take away the taxpayer's real property (a process known as condemnation), the taxpayer is entitled to fair compensation. The taxpayer is usually given cash in return for the condemned property. The taxpayer may occasionally get property other than cash. When the sum obtained from the government exceeds the adjusted basis in the condemned property, taxpayers profit. They incur a loss when the amount received is less than the property's adjusted basis.

Taxpayers would pay tax on all recognized profits resulting from condemnations under the general rule, but may deduct losses solely on condemned business or investment property. Even though it is an unavoidable event, there is no deduction for condemnation losses on personal-use property.

Gains and Losses as a Result of Casualty or Theft

When the value of the loss exceeds the amount compensated by insurance, taxpayers experience a casualty or theft loss. For personal-use property and partially damaged commercial or investment property, the loss is equal to the smaller of (i) the property's adjusted basis or (ii) its drop in FMV.

The difference between the FMV before and after the casualty or theft is used to calculate the FMV decline. Even if the drop in FMV is less, the amount of the loss for entirely destroyed (including stolen) commercial or investment property matches the adjusted basis in the property.

The taxpayer does not recognize a casualty or theft loss where the insurance proceeds exceed the amount of the loss. Instead, a casualty or theft gain is realized by the taxpayer when the insurance proceeds exceed the taxpayer's adjusted basis in the property.

Taxpayers often recognize both income and losses from tragedy or theft incidents. The unique rules for computing the itemized deduction for casualty or theft losses on personal-use items were covered in Chapter 5. It should be emphasized that the only deductible losses that an individual can claim on personal-use items are casualty and theft losses.

Election to Postpone Recognition of Realized Gains

Taxpayers generally recognize gains on property involved in an involuntary conversion. But, taxpayers can defer these profits provided they invest the whole amount in qualifying replacement property within a certain time frame. If the taxpayer receives cash in exchange for the converted property, this provision is optional. If the option is chosen, taxpayers will recognize a gain (up to the amount of realized gain) on sums not reinvested.

> The local government condemns Daniel's property. The government pays Daniel $200,000 for the property. The property has an adjusted basis of $170,000. Daniel can avoid recognizing the $30,000 realized gain ($200,000 − $170,000) if he reinvests at least $200,000 in qualified replacement property within the required time period.

When taxpayers opt to postpone profits, the amount of postponed gain is deducted from the taxpayer's basis in the new property. Assuming Craig from Example 46 purchases eligible replacement property for $190,000, he will realize a $10,000 gain ($200,000 $190,000) and can choose to defer the remainder ($30,000 $10,000 = $20,000). Craig's basis in the qualifying replacement property would be $170,000 ($190,000 purchase price less $20,000 deferred gain).

Qualified Replacement Property
Qualified replacement property is often property linked in service or usage for property engaged in an involuntary conversion. As a result, taxpayers are frequently required to replace an office building with another office building. Similarly, they must replace equipment with comparable functional equipment. This rule does have two exceptions
.

The first exemption pertains to taxpayers who lease out involuntary conversion property. For these taxpayers, qualified replacement property entails investing in other rental property. It is not necessary for the rental property to be of the same type. As a result, taxpayers who lease out an office building that was damaged in a catastrophe might replace it with an apartment building or any other rental property that they lease out.

The second exemption permits taxpayers to replace condemned commercial or investment real estate with any other commercial or investment real estate. Taxpayers can replace a condemned office building with investment land. Instead, they may replace it with an apartment complex, a warehouse, or any other type of commercial or investment property.

Replacement Period

A taxpayer who realizes a gain through an involuntary conversion might defer the gain by replacing the converted property within a certain time frame. The time of replacement begins on the day the property was damaged, destroyed, or stolen. The time for condemned property begins when the government publicly threatens to condemn the property.

Taxpayers typically have two years following the end of the tax year (December 31 for calendar year taxpayers) to complete the purchase of the qualifying replacement property. Taxpayers who have had their commercial or investment real estate condemned by the government have an additional year (for a total of three years) to purchase qualifying replacement property.

On October 19, 20x1, Desmond's business property was completely destroyed in a fire. At the time of the fire, the property was worth $40,000. Desmond paid $80,000 for the property 20 years earlier, and its adjusted basis at the time of the fire was $30,000. In 20x2, the insurance company paid Desmond $40,000. Desmons's business casualty gain equals $10,000 ($40,000 − $30,000 adjusted basis). If he wants to postpone the entire gain, he must reinvest at least $40,000 in qualified replacement property between October 19, 20x1, and December 31, 20x3 (two years after the year in which Desmond receives the proceeds and realizes the gain).

Same facts as above, except that the business property was condemned and in 20x1 the government paid Desmond $40,000 for the property. To avoid recognition of any of the $10,000 gain, Desmond has from the date on which the government notified him of the condemnation until December 31, 20x4 (three years after 20x1) to buy qualified replacement property costing at least $40,000.

Taxpayers whose primary residence is destroyed in a federally declared disaster region have an additional two years to reinvest in qualifying replacement property. In effect, this allows them until December 31 of the fourth year following the year in which they realize a gain to invest in another property that they use as their primary residence.

The Jesse's main home was badly damaged by fire in a federally declared disaster area. They received $820,000 from their insurance company in 20x1. The jesse's basis in the home is $270,000. In order to postpone the entire $550,000 gain realized in 20x1 ($820,000 − $270,000 adjusted basis), they have until December 31, 20x4 (four years after 20x1, the year the proceeds were received and the gain was first realized) to use the $820,000 proceeds to buy (or build) a new main home.

Chapter 8

Asset and Protection in Marriage and Divorce

If you are married, as most of us are, divorce might be the greatest danger to your assets. Nonetheless, it is remarkable how few individuals plan financially for what is likely to be the most important choice of their life.

According to a 2010 report in USA Today, less than 5% of all married persons have a marital property agreement. With the time and attention we invest into finding and courting our partners, as well as the possible financial concerns at play, it's surprising that so few of us take the time to financially plan for this most crucial element of our lives. Those who have been through acrimonious divorces—with each spouse digging into the other's financial and personal affairs, paying investigators to unearth whatever dirt they can use as leverage in child custody, property division, alimony, and so on— have understood the costs of neglecting to plan. Furthermore, many couples are unaware that a marital property agreement may be a critical asset protection tool that shields both spouses from third-party creditors.

Who is the owner of what?

Property obtained by couples during a marriage is generally considered joint property of the spouses.

This is known as "common property." This is called "community property" in community property states and "marital property" in common law states. For this chapter, I'll use the term "marital property."

All property obtained by one spouse during the marriage (e.g., earnings, real estate, securities, retirement savings, etc.) is deemed marital property unless it can be traced back to separate property, as explained below. Earnings gained during marriage are a frequent example of marital property.

MARITAL PROPERTY AGREEMENTS
Prenuptial and postnuptial agreements are both considered marital property agreements, and they need to include specific terms and be executed under certain conditions to be valid. Regrettably, a couple can't simply sit down by themselves and sign an agreement regarding the finances in their marriage. They must consult with separate attorneys.

COMMUNITY PROPERTY VS. COMMON LAW
Early in the history of our country, a few states adopted a legal principle called "community property."

Essentially, in a community property state, if a property is acquired during marriage, it will be presumed community property unless an effort is made to designate it as sole and separate property. Thus, joint equal ownership is automatically presumed by law in the absence of specific evidence. In common law states, property isn't automatically presumed to be "community," or equally shared. Thus, property titled in the name of one spouse or acquired by just one spouse may be treated as separate property, and must go through a separate analysis to determine whether it is marital property.

Every other property is typically considered "separate property," including inheritance and property acquired before marriage by a spouse. Also, the money earned by the distinct property is kept separate. As a result, if you inherit a rental property from your parents, the rentals from that unit are often considered distinct property. Of course, whether the assets are commingled with marital property affects the overall norm (see below).

The Dangers of Co-mingling

Many people are unaware that, while property may enter the marriage as separate property (e.g., a rental owned by one spouse prior to the marriage) or be acquired during the marriage (e.g., an inheritance), the character of some or all of the property can change during the marriage based on the behavior of the spouses.

For example, if a woman had a rental previous to the marriage but used her weekly income to remodel it during the marriage, most states would consider all or a portion of the redesign to be marital property because the wife paid for it with marital property (i.e., her paycheck). But, if the wife can show that the remodel was paid for with rent (which is separate property), the remodel will remain her separate property.

Many people do not account for their separate and married assets and have no awareness of the necessity of, much alone a plan for, keeping the two separate. Actually, combining separate and marital property is the most typical error spouses make throughout their marriage. If the woman put her rent checks into the same bank account as she deposited her salary in the renovation scenario above, she would be commingling her independent property (rent checks) with her marital property (wages). If she subsequently used a check from this account to pay the remodel, she would be unable to explain that the money originated from her rent checks rather than her salary, and the redesign would most likely be regarded a marital asset.

Furthermore, if the husband's creditors attempted to seize the wife's bank account, she would have a tough time proving that the account is her distinct property if she had been depositing her salary in it for years. It is critical to establish separate accounts for marital and separate assets for asset protection purposes.

Rules in a Community Property State

In community property states, the manner of retaining title has no bearing on whether the property is marital or separate. Many individuals in common property jurisdictions, for example, believe that if they title property acquired after marriage in their name as "sole and separate property," it is separate property. Not necessarily. You'll need more specific, documented evidence of this desire.

Hence, in a community property state, property gained after marriage is deemed to be common property. During a divorce, the court will consider whether the spouse claiming a separate property interest can demonstrate that he or she followed the stated requirements to convert community property to separate property (this is called a transmutation). Transmutations are governed by state laws. Always consult your attorney to ascertain the appropriate conditions for a transmutation, and consult your CPA on any potential tax repercussions.

Arizona, California, Idaho, Louisiana, Nevada, New Mexico, Texas, Washington, and Wisconsin are the nine community property states, and it's critical to understand how their distinct regulations might effect your possessions. While Alaska is not a community property state, it does enable couples to enter into a community property arrangement; property remains separate until both partners agree to make it community property via a community property agreement or a community property trust.

However, it should be noted that in 2021, Tennessee became the first state to pass legislation allowing for the creation of "beneficiary deeds" for real property. Beneficiary deeds allow for the transfer of real property to a named beneficiary upon the owner's death, without the need for probate. This could potentially impact the division of assets in the event of divorce or death, so it's important for individuals in Tennessee to consider this when planning their estate or going through a divorce.

Division of Property in Common Law States

Property named in the name of one spouse is considered distinct property in common law states. As a result, asset protection from creditors generally includes placing the asset in the name of the spouse who is least at risk. Nonetheless, in a divorce, the property will still be divided based on whether it is considered marital or separate property, according to the basic characterization principles I've already outlined.

In these states, the court normally divides marital property equally unless it is inequitable to do so. But, judges have broad discretion in determining what is equitable in any specific scenario and may consider considerations such as age, health, prospective income, and asset value. Some courts also consider marital wrongdoing (infidelity, domestic violence, etc.) to be important factors.

This is what makes divorce courts so frightening. What a court considers equitable may differ greatly from what you consider equitable, and who has the title has less of an influence than you might imagine when determining how property is distributed in a divorce. This is why, before appearing in front of a divorce court judge, you should make these decisions on your own utilizing a marital property agreement.

Making a Legal Marriage Contract

To safeguard your assets, marital agreements, whether prenuptial or postnuptial, are critical and must adhere to technical regulations. If the requirements for writing and entering into the agreement are not followed, they will do nothing to safeguard the parties and their assets from one other after a divorce.

The rules differ from state to state, so make sure you have an attorney create or at least evaluate your marital agreement.

Some of the standards that states require for a legal marital property agreement include:

1. Each party must retain their own counsel to advise them on their rights and responsibilities under the marital agreement.

2. Each spouse must offer complete disclosure of their assets and liabilities prior to entering into the agreement so that each spouse is fully aware.

3. The parties should always be given enough time and space to think about the conditions of the agreement. Any claim that

If the bargaining process was unfair, the agreement might be declared void. Several courts, for example, will not enforce prenuptial agreements signed into at the eleventh hour before the marriage.

Prenuptial and postnuptial agreements

A postnuptial agreement is a legal agreement between spouses that outlines how assets and liabilities will be divided in the event of a divorce or legal separation. Unlike a prenuptial agreement, which is signed before marriage, a postnuptial agreement is signed during the marriage.

A postnuptial agreement should be considered in situations where there has been a significant change in circumstances during the marriage, such as the acquisition of new assets, a change in financial status, or the birth of children. It can also be considered when one spouse inherits a significant amount of money or assets during the marriage, or when one spouse has a business that they want to protect in the event of a divorce.

A postnuptial agreement can cover a wide range of topics, including the division of property, alimony or spousal support, and the distribution of assets upon death. It can also address issues related to debt, taxes, and retirement benefits.

Postnuptial agreements are enforced in the same way as prenuptial agreements. They must be in writing and signed by both parties. Each party must have the opportunity to review the agreement with an attorney before signing. Postnuptial agreements may be subject to legal challenges if they are found to be unfair or if they were signed under duress or coercion. It is important to have a knowledgeable attorney draft the agreement and to ensure that both parties fully understand the terms of the agreement before signing.

Using Irrevocable Trusts to Avoid Marital Planning

Some people delay having the prenuptial agreement debate in order to safeguard their assets from divorce without damaging a relationship or creating an embarrassing scenario. This is where an irrevocable trust might come in handy for someone who is thinking about getting married soon.

In general, trusts can be revocable, which means that the person who creates the trust has the ability to withdraw the trust. Yet, an irrevocable trust is one that cannot be revoked by the person who created it. As a result, an irrevocable trust may be a useful instrument for removing assets from your estate, making them inaccessible to creditors or a divorcing spouse.

If you transfer assets to an irrevocable trust before a future marriage, the assets become the trust's property rather than yours. But, one important disadvantage is that you may lose a large amount of control and benefit enjoyment of the property. There may also be gift tax implications. As a result, you should consult with both your attorney and your CPA about the benefits and drawbacks of creating an irrevocable trust for future marriage planning.

Game Plan Takeaway

It's easy to remain in denial about the possibility of divorce, but we must be realistic. Researchers agree that determining the divorce rate in the United States is difficult, but we do know it is far too high and traumatic when it occurs. When it comes to marriage, estate, and asset protection planning, don't overlook the prospect of divorce.

In conclusion, understanding how to protect your assets in marriage and divorce is crucial for your financial well-being. Whether you are getting married or are already married, it's important to take proactive steps to protect your assets. This can include taking measures such as creating prenuptial or postnuptial agreements, understanding community property laws, and properly titling assets.

Additionally, it's important to continually reassess and update your asset protection strategies as circumstances change, such as the acquisition of new assets or changes in marital status. This will help ensure that your asset protection plan remains effective and relevant over time.

Overall, taking proactive steps to protect your assets can be a key component of overall financial planning and can help provide a solid foundation for your financial future.

Afterword

Taking Control of Your Taxes

Congratulations! You have made it through the Savvy Tax Payer Playbook and now have a better understanding of the US tax system and how to navigate it to your advantage. By understanding tax structures, deductions, exemptions, and reporting procedures, you have the tools to save money on your taxes and avoid any pitfalls that might lead to an audit.

Remember that the US tax code is complex and ever-changing, so it's important to stay up-to-date on any changes that might affect your tax situation. Consult with a tax professional if you have any questions or concerns about your taxes. They can help you make the most of your deductions and credits, and can provide valuable guidance on how to minimize your tax liability.

By taking control of your taxes, you can save money and achieve your financial goals. Whether it's saving for retirement, paying for education, or starting a business, the tax code offers a range of incentives and opportunities to help you succeed. With the knowledge and strategies you have gained from this book, you can confidently navigate the tax system and make the most of your hard-earned money.

Remember, the key to successful tax planning is to be proactive and stay informed. By staying on top of your tax situation, you can avoid surprises and ensure that you are always in compliance with the tax code. With the Savvy Tax Payer Playbook as your guide, you can take control of your taxes and build a brighter financial future. Good luck, and happy tax planning!

THE END

Request for Review

If you found this book beneficial, I would appreciate it if you could provide an honest review on the Amazon website. Your help is greatly appreciated and makes a significant difference.

I personally read all of the reviews in order to gain realistic feedback on how I can make adjustments and modifications that will help future readers.

It's really simple to leave a review if you feel so inclined. All you have to do is go to the Amazon page for this book and click on the *"leave a customer review"* button - this will take you directly to the review section.

I am grateful for your assistance.

Sincere Regards

Mack

Glossary of Terms

Adjusted Gross Income (AGI): The amount of income a taxpayer has after subtracting allowable deductions.

Basis: The cost of an asset for tax purposes, used to calculate gains or losses on the asset
.

Capital gain: A profit made from the sale of a capital asset, such as stocks or real estate.

Depreciation: A decrease in the value of an asset over time due to wear and tear, obsolescence, or other factors.

Estate tax: A tax on the transfer of property from a deceased person's estate to their heirs or beneficiaries.

Gross income: The total amount of income received before any deductions or taxes are taken out
.

Inheritance tax: A tax on the transfer of property or assets from a deceased person to their heirs or beneficiaries.

Itemized deduction: A deduction taken on personal income tax returns for specific expenses, such as medical expenses, charitable contributions, and mortgage interest.

Modified Adjusted Gross Income (MAGI): AGI with certain deductions added back in.

Non-deductible IRA: An individual retirement account in which contributions are not tax-deductible but withdrawals in retirement are tax-free.

Roth IRA: An individual retirement account in which contributions are made after-tax, but withdrawals in retirement are tax-free.

Standard deduction: A set amount of deduction allowed for certain taxpayers based on their filing status and other factors, without the need for itemized deductions.

Tax bracket: The range of income levels at which different tax rates apply.

Withholding: The amount of income tax deducted from a paycheck or other income before it is received by the taxpayer.

www.ingramcontent.com/pod-product-compliance
Lightning Source LLC
Chambersburg PA
CBHW071134220526
45467CB00015B/987